GOING VEGAN

Acknowlegements

There are several people I would like to thank for helping make this book happen. Firstly, I would like to thank my wife, Samantha, for her endless encouragement throughout its creation. For tasting every single recipe and letting me know, in no uncertain terms, if the dishes weren't good enough. She has been patient and kind from beginning to end and has blessed me with her constant support and enthusiasm.

I would like to thank my children, Katherine, Charlotte and Morgan, for bearing with my absence during the writing of this book, and for enduring my constant use of the kitchen.

I am also grateful to the many tasters, who participated in making Going Vegan. Samantha, of course. Katherine Griffin, Charlotte Griffin, Graham Horne, June Noakes, Nicola Cross (for making my own recipe and serving it to me for breakfast), Ebony Church, James Cross (who loved those pancakes), Russ Church, Stacey Hawkins, Emma Hawkins, Momo Medina Vilches, Denise Law, Sarah Acheng.

I would like to thank my family in Cardiff, Russ and Sheila Church, Nicola, Andrew and her family, Jacqueline and Ebony, for their constant support.

Thanks also the Petra and the team at Stockfood and Shelley and the team at Alamy for the use of the stock images.

All of you have helped make the dream of this book become a reality, and I am eternally grateful.

WANT MORE RECIPES?

Visit my blog at: www.richardchurchphoto.com/blog

See me on Facebook: @richardchurchuk

This book is for Samantha, who daily changes my life for the better.

CONTENTS

INTRODUCTION

This is not just a book for vegans, or even those thinking of becoming vegan. It *is* for you, of course, but it is also a book for anyone who would like to introduce more plant-based eating into their diet, who would like to cut down on their animal food intake and increase the amount of vegetables they put into their bodies. Going vegan is, in my opinion, one of the best personal journeys a person can undertake. It permanently alters the way we think about food and the way we eat for the better. But even if you are only going vegan a couple of days a week, this book is still for you.

Within these pages you will find little bits of advice to help you navigate various stumbling blocks when it comes to plant-based eating. There are tips on shopping, on filling your store cupboard, as well as on the basics of cooking, if all that is new to you. There is also some advice on making healthier eating choices to help you avoid those boxes of frozen, ready-made dinners wherever possible. Most importantly, there are recipes. One hundred and fourteen plant-based dishes that, I hope, will get you cooking things you've never tried before, as well as new takes on meals you might be more familiar with.

The recipes are organised into breakfast, lunch and dinner, as well as sections on sauces, side dishes and desserts. I've also included a small part on cooking the essentials, which you can refer to throughout your use of this book. If cooking is a completely alien concept to you, or even if you just need a refresher, then I have covered the basic cooking techniques at the beginning for you to either study, or browse over at your leisure.

That's the book. Now here's a little about me.

In the spring of 2014 I made a spur-of-the-moment decision that would completely change the course of my life. I was a voracious meat-eater. Though I enjoyed food of all kinds I was, like many meat eaters, a little put out by the thought of a meal without it. Though my wife, Samantha, was vegetarian and had been since I'd known her, her distaste for animal flesh had not rubbed off on me. If we went out to eat, I didn't even consider the vegetarian option but went straight for what I believed was the good stuff. It was the same at home. I cooked two separate meals rather than go without meat.

About a year before the spring of 2014 I started getting some dietary problems, which turned out to be a lactose intolerance. I tried, with only moderate effort and a number of failures, to go dairy-free. What I had settled for was *almost* dairy-free, which meant I still ate pizza and didn't spend too much time reading the ingredients of things. This, of course, didn't do too much to improve my health and I was still experiencing problems. Then, on that particularly sunny spring afternoon, I ate a meat pie at my favourite restaurant and was ill not long after. I turned to Samantha and said: 'I think I'm going to try to go vegan.'

She nodded her approval and expected, as I did, that this new venture would last until my discomfort subsided and I walked past the next burger bar. To both of our surprise, I am still vegan nearly four years on. My wife joined me a year later and we are both happily living on a plant-based diet.

If you're reading this book I shall assume that you have also made the decision to, at least in some part, turn to veganism. Perhaps you have been for some time, perhaps this is all new to you or maybe you are not there yet but are either considering changing over, or would simply like to add more vegan options into your diet. Wherever you are on this journey you should be proud of yourself for being open to what is a very clean and enjoyable way of living.

I have always cooked, right from making my first pizza at the age of thirteen. I would follow Antonio Carluccio's classic pizza recipe and repeat it over and over, until I got it right. When I was twenty-two I decided to try cooking for a living, starting at the bottom and learning on the job. I did this for more than ten years before trying my hand at photography. When I went vegan I had to relearn. I had to find a different way of doing things. I was as obsessed with good food as I had always been, but I suddenly found myself with (or so I thought at the time) less ingredients to play with and, although many of the rules of cooking still applied, there were different techniques that I had to get my head around. So I read, I worked, and I experimented. I made a lot of mistakes, but that is how we learn.

This book is the end result of that learning. It contains the information that I've come across in my time as a vegan, as well as solutions to the problems that I have faced. It contains the recipes that I have put together over that time, from 'veganising' everyday dishes to coming up with something completely new. This is the food that I enjoy making and love eating. I hope you will get the same pleasure out of them that I have.

A QUICK WORD ABOUT GLUTEN-FREE RECIPES

This book is 100 per cent plant-based. Not only that, but the vast majority of the recipes are also gluten-free. I am not gluten-intolerant myself, but I have tried to make the book as inclusive as possible so that everyone can enjoy the food.

Recipes that are gluten-free I have labelled as such at the top of the ingredients column. I have also listed those that are easy to convert to gluten-free by simply switching an ingredient or two.

For practical reasons I have labelled oats as gluten-free, as it is only the production practices that make them unsuitable for people with coeliac disease or severe intolerances. If this is the case for you, then make sure you buy oats that are labelled gluten-free on their packaging.

Congratulations! You've Made the Decision to go Vegan

You've thought long and hard about it. You've weighed up the pros and cons. You've watched all the grizzly videos on social media, and now finally you've made the decision: This is it. You're going to become vegan.

Firstly, I salute you. Take a moment to think about the enormity of your decision, the positive repercussions it will have on your health, as well as on the planet in general. This is enormous. You should be proud.

You are about to embark on the greatest food adventure of your life. Not only will you enjoy incredible health benefits from your new diet, you will also be able to appreciate everything you eat, knowing that you have not contributed to animal suffering in order to get great-tasting food. You are in for many pleasant surprises along your journey, particularly if you are an adventurous cook (and I do hope you are). New and often astounding taste combinations are now open to you. Ways of doing things that you might never have thought of before making this decision, that you might not have even considered possible. There's a lot to learn, but take it one step at a time and you'll be enjoying a happy and fulfilling vegan lifestyle before you know it.

Now you've decided to do this you've got to make a few changes, and one of the major areas in need of adjustment is your store cupboard. Have a look at yours. Go on, I'll wait.

What have you got there? Some mayonnaise, a few tins of ravioli, some ketchup. Someone hasn't been shopping for a while. Now, a couple of those things are probably going to have to go. When I say 'go', I don't mean put at the back of the cupboard, in the section labelled only eat in an emergency! I mean so long, farewell. It's time to remove the safety net. At this point I feel I must say, don't grab everything non-vegan off the shelf and throw them onto an open fire, dancing triumphantly around the burning embers or your former lifestyle. If you're not going to eat it anymore, give the food to a friend or family member. Better yet, donate it to your local food bank.

Now that your shelf is clear, you need to start filling it up again with things that are animal-free. Seems like one hell of a task, right? Well... yes. At least at the beginning.

The trick is to take small steps. Changing what you eat does not necessarily mean starting again from scratch. Try adjusting to vegan versions of things you used to eat anyway. You like pancakes on a Saturday morning? Don't panic. Vegan pancakes are no more challenging to make than the ones you're used to. Bolognese was your Tuesday night staple? No reason why it can't still be. You just switch your meat mince for veg mince. A word of caution when changing to veggie products: Not all of them are vegan. Eggs and milk are quite abundant in vegetarian ready-made food, even ones that don't seem immediately obvious. A couple of vegetarian minces contain egg. At the time of writing Tesco's own brand frozen veggie mince contains no egg or milk and is very easy to use (just pour it into your sauce ten minutes before the end). There are some very good dried minces available online, which I use almost exclusively now, as they are also gluten-free and my daughter is coeliac. www.realfoods. co.uk is where I go for mine. Chilli is also an easy switch. You can see my recipe for some seriously good chilli on page 184.

Try making a list of the things you like eating now. We're all creatures of habit and tend to eat the same things often. Write them down, then you can see what changes you need to make for them to be vegan. Often, it's only a few changes.

Cheese

The selection of vegan cheese available now is nothing short of astounding, and it seems that new varieties are added with increasing speed.

Until recently, getting vegan cheese to melt like dairy cheese was something of a challenge, but there have been some great improvements of late and now there are a few that will melt perfectly for pizzas, or whatever else you have in mind. My wife and I still buy most of our cheese from specialist online suppliers, but the supermarkets are getting much better at meeting the demand. At the time of writing Tesco has at least twelve varieties of vegan cheese and Sainsbury's stock eleven. I'm sure that, by the time you read this, those numbers will have increased.

The versatility of these cheeses ranges greatly. Jeezo do a 400g block that is really good for melting, but has quite a mild flavour if you prefer more strength and character. It does come in a decent size, however, so it's a good all-rounder for the family. At home, it is our main go-to cheese, used in sauces, on pizza, or for sandwiches. Jeezo is available at www.vegancheese.co.uk. Violife's Prosociano is a hard Italian cheese alternative that is outstanding and Sainsbury's own vegan cream cheese means you'll never again be far away from a good bagel.

When I first started out I was a little disappointed with the vegan cheese alternatives I was eating, but that is no longer the case. The breadth of range available now means that there is something for everybody to enjoy and to suit just about every dish. Try a couple of them. If one isn't to your taste, don't be put off. There are many more out there to sample.

Tofu

Although being vegan is not all tofu-eating, as some might have you believe, it is certainly a powerful tool to have in your arsenal. Tofu is typically the protein of choice for vegetarians and vegans, containing anything from 12-20g of protein per 100g of product. Though it is far from your only source, it is a good place to start when switching from a meat-based diet.

Tofu has a lot of uses. You can pan-fry it with spices when making a curry. It can be cooked with nutritional yeast and gram flour to make the vegan alternative to scrambled eggs (see page 68). It can be blended into quiches or tarts (page 219), and even used in chocolate mousse (page 245). Tofu comes mainly in block and silken varieties, which differ in density depending on the one you buy. It can be bought sitting in water, marinated or smoked (which is extra firm and particularly delightful), and you can even buy it seasoned, diced and ready-cooked, either to stir-fry or eat as it is. I've included a number of tofu recipes in this book, which I hope will demonstrate its versatility.

Fresh Produce

Stocking your fridge with delicious fresh fruit and vegetables is an unbeatable way to fully embrace the vegan diet, and will certainly help you to move beyond the cabbages and peas you grew up with. There are some vegetables that I would consider a must in a vegan diet, such as avocados, spinach, cherry tomatoes, aubergines and, of course, kale. If you're new to the seemingly endless array of fruit and veg out there, then choosing what to get might seem a little daunting. My advice would be to pick a recipe you like the look of and start with the vegetables for that. Like what you're eating? Get the same things again, only this time branch out to one or two other items. What I wouldn't recommend is filling your fridge so full that half of what you buy ends up going in the bin. Take it slow to start, and minimise your waste by only buying what you're sure you're going to use.

Vegetables are, and should be, the centre point of a vegan meal. When I'm cooking, I tend to start with the vegetables I want to use and then work from there. Of course, that can sometimes translate as 'what vegetables need using up in the fridge before I have to throw them out?' which is a question that can still lead to some quite creative cooking.

It is horrifyingly easy to be an unhealthy vegan. There are countless sugar and fat-ridden traps to fall into, making it all too easy to forget the benefits of a vegan diet, which is healthy eating. We all transgress, and I try to atone for my sins with other, more wisely-considered food choices throughout the week. This is where vegetables, and a good variety of vegetables at that, play an important role. If you're already a seasoned veggie-eater, then keep at it. If you're typically a green food avoider, then it's time to get your feet wet, or at least dip your toes in the water for the time being

The recipes provided here encompass a large selection of fruit and veg, legumes and seeds for all tastes, to give as balanced a diet as possible, using ingredients that are easy to find and will get you creatively cooking. Many of the dishes are gluten free, some naturally but others by choice, in order to make the book as inclusive as possible. It is my hope that making these dishes will give you as much variety of fruit and veg as possible, so that, not only will you be eating more healthily, but you'll also never be stuck in a rut at dinner time again.

ADVICE FOR NEW VEGANS

According to research conducted on behalf of The Vegan Society, over half a million people in the UK have now made the switch to a plant-based diet. Not only that, but January 2018 saw 150, 000 people signing up to Veganuary, smashing their previous record. There is no doubt that veganism is on the rise, with not only animal welfare concerns but increased media attention to meat-attributing environmental issues encouraging former omnivores to ditch animal products altogether in favour of a more herbivorous regime.

For some, giving up meat and dairy can be a relatively smooth transition, whereas others find the change a lot more challenging. Common foods to cling to are cheese, eggs and chocolate and a lot of would-be vegans find it hard to let these go. My own journey was made a little easier by becoming lactose intolerant long before I decided to give veganism a try, so I was not consuming much dairy to begin with. My wife, on the other hand was a self-confessed cheese addict and that was the one area that made her journey problematic. How did she deal with it? She bought a huge online consignment of vegan cheese, containing just about every variety one could imagine. A comfy blanket, if you will, to cling to on the road ahead.

As I've said previously, vegan cheeses vary greatly in texture, taste and the way they cook. They don't all melt like regular cheese, but many do and now have similar properties to their dairy counterparts. There is enough variety on the market for you to pick any number of cheeses that you will enjoy greatly. I have been making pizzas, nachos and other melting cheese dishes using these products for a few years now and am perfectly satisfied with the results.

There is now an abundance of alternatives to dairy cheese and, by shopping online, you can have them delivered straight to your door. Here's a selection of the stores, in addition to the supermarkets, that my family use to get our cheeses, as well as many other vegan products:

www.veggiestuff.com
www.goodnessdirect.co.uk
www.thevegankind.com
www.alternativestores.com
www.vegancheese.co.uk
www.realfoods.co.uk

Of course, there are other questions that cause concern for the vegan newbie. One that is asked most often by family and friends when you announce for desire to go vegan is: 'How are you going to get your protein?'

For the newcomer, this question can cause some alarm. How *am* I going to get my protein? You may ask yourself. The answer is simple: eat a balanced, healthy diet and you will have all the protein you need. There is plenty of protein, complex carbohydrates and fibre in a plant-based diet, providing you are eating healthily. Let's take broccoli for example. There are 2.8 grams of protein per 100g of broccoli. Spinach had 2.9 grams and 4.3 grams in the same amount of kale. Legumes have a higher percentage of protein, with peas reaching 5 grams per 100 and boiled chickpeas a whopping 9 grams. Braised tofu, incidentally, had 14.2 grams. It comes in a can and is extremely diverse when it comes to cooking. I get mine from Holland and Barret and, if you are looking for some ideas, why not try my Vegan Braised Tofu Thai Cakes on page 96. To make good use of peas, try my Spaghetti with Coriander and Pea Pesto, which also contains spinach (page 174).

Another initial challenge for the beginning vegan is the store cupboard. It is easy to be put off by the constant reading of labels when shopping at the supermarket, but in truth this only lasts for a short while and is actually a great exercise in making us aware of what we are putting into our bodies on a daily basis. The fact is that we, as human beings, are creatures of habit and that extends to our grocery shopping. Once we've got our cupboards stocked up with the things we like we tend to get those things repeatedly, removing the need to constantly read labels.

On the subject of label-reading, vitamin B12 is a serious issue for vegans and is the only vitamin that cannot be consumed within a healthy plant-based diet. Many foods such as milks and cereals are now fortified with

B12. Vegan yogurts also contain a small amount. While it is possible to get sufficient B12 in this manner, it is certainly more convenient to take a quality vitamin B12 supplement. According to The Vegan Society a daily dose of at least 10 micrograms is sufficient for our requirements, so one 500 micrograms tablet each day is more than adequate. It is also a good idea to pay attention to E numbers on food labels, as some are derived from shelfish, beetles and milk. A quick search online will tell you which ones to avoid.

For those taking the plunge, there are certainly challenges ahead, but none of them are insurmountable. The biggest hurdle is probably eating out, but more and more restaurants are now acknowledging veganism on their menus. If you've never been there before, calling your chosen eatery ahead of time is a good way of finding out if you're going to have a satisfying meal. Some restaurants are prepared for vegans and some are not, but it has been my experience that you can find something to eat at most places. Chefs are nearly always happy to make a more bespoke meal, providing they have the ingredients in stock and you have not turned up at the busiest time. You might find that you can eat some things off the vegetarian menu if certain items, such as cheese or mayonnaise, are excluded. One place I go to has a sweet potato and halloumi burger, where I get them to substitute the halloumi for mushrooms to make it vegan. This kind of eating out gets you by in a whole number of places and will certainly do on an impromptu restaurant visit. The good news is that restaurant menus are changing all the time. With veganism becoming ever more popular, eateries seem to be adapting almost as quickly. There will always be some who lag behind, but I think the future is definitely bright for those of us who enjoy dining out.

In the beginning the journey into veganism can seem difficult, the road full of potholes and endless No Entry signs. The good news is that the initial struggles are short-lived. Once veganism becomes your way of life you will not be able to imagine how you could have lived any other way. For your health, for the health of the environment and for all other beings, it is a journey worth taking.

THE VEGAN STORE CUPBOARD IN DETAIL

By now you are aware that there are a number of foodstuffs you have chosen to no longer eat. That jar of mayonnaise we talked about earlier, for example, contains egg and sometimes milk products. It's probably the same for your favourite packet of biscuits, and let's not even get started on the vast array of chocolate bars you will no longer be consuming. But this is looking at the glass half empty. You have the opportunity here to fill your shelves with a wonderful array of new and exciting products. Almond butter, tahini, tamari, semolina flour and pulses of all varieties, and the list goes on.

Modern-day veganism, thanks largely to social media and the internet as a whole, is vastly more accessible than it used to be. New products are being added on an almost daily basis, and the more people there are who desire these products, the more there will be. This once exclusive and rather isolated club is getting bigger and bigger, and slipping more and more into the mainstream. It is far easier to get hold of items now than it has ever been, even at your local supermarket. The current rather impressive cheese selection in a lot of supermarkets is proof of that. Tofu is available everywhere (despite my father having never heard of it when I mentioned it to him recently) and is also sold in many varieties. Mainstream restaurants are now beginning to offer more vegan options on their menus and pizza places are finally giving us dairy-free cheese. The world is changing fast and for the better as far as a plant-based diet is concerned.

So, the question becomes: with all of these choices now available to us, at do we stock up on?

The answer to this, I believe, is to take it slow and steady. It's tempting to get your hands on every new thing you can, but your shopping bill will soon mount up if you do it this way. My advice is to start with a few new items and then build up from there. If you've never had tofu before, or don't fully understand what you are doing with it yet, then get the plain tofu. I always have the one that's soaked in water in my fridge, as it's the one I use the most. There are a number of recipes for it in this book. We also keep a tofu that's cut and ready to eat for nights when we don't want too much fuss. Pre-packed tofu has a fairly long shelf life, so you can get a couple in at a time.

Some things are fairly simple to trade up. Mayonnaise can be bought in the Free-From section of the larger supermarkets for about £1.50 (I also have a recipe for it on page 58). You can usually find a vegan chocolate spread there too, which has become a bit of a staple in my house. Some items are just vegan anyway. Peanut butter, for example, as well as jams and marmalade. It doesn't hurt, however, to check the labels to make sure there are no surprises. There are a number of dairy-free spreads available now. I use Pure, but Flora do one as well, as do Vitalite. If you want to get fancy there are a number of nut-based butters, mostly cashew, that you can try, though you will have to spend more money for less. I usually reserve these for a dish where the butter is going to be more prominent, say for a jacket potato.

There are an excellent variety of dairy-free milks within easy reach. Soya, almond, coconut, rice, oat and hazelnut are the most commonly sold. Each of them have their uses, and personal taste will dictate which one you use most often. I have found over time that I didn't have much of a taste for soya milk, and so my main go-to had become almond. I often use rice and hazelnut for deserts, as they suit them so well. Hazelnut is quite a dark and sweet milk that is, in my opinion, not suitable for making coffee with. But it does produce and excellent rice pudding!

One company that makes a lot of good dairy-free products is Alpro, though this brand doesn't appear to be in all territories. I've had conversation with a few Australians who say it isn't available over there. We can only hope that this changes in the near future.

I've created a list of what I consider to be store cupboard essentials. The list is not all-inclusive, but rather a guide to the items that I have at home, and that you will need to cook the recipes in this book.

Flours

I use a variety of flours in my cooking. From simple plain and self-raising flour, to wholemeal, spelt and rye flours. There are gluten-free flours that I use as well, both to be more inclusive in my recipes and because my daughter is coeliac. These again have a plain and self-raising variety. My personal favourite is buckwheat, which you will see used a bit in this book, but I also like to use gram flour for a few recipes. Coconut and soya flour also appear here.

Other flours I use are semolina and maize flour, or polenta.

The chances are that you already have some of these flours to hand and my advice is to get the ones you need for each recipe as you are making them. Just keep them stored in an air-tight container. Soya flour is best stored in the fridge after opening to stop it turning bitter.

Pasta

In my opinion whole wheat pasta is always more preferable to white pasta. It takes a little longer to cook but has more flavour and bite to it. Plus the fibre content is higher. You can get whole wheat versions of quite a few of the pasta shapes out there and I would recommend trying them if you haven't done so already. The standard gluten-free versions tend to be a bit bland, so I would recommend looking a bit further afield. Neapolitan do a very nice pasta made from pea flour, which I use in this book, and there are also pastas made from lentils and quinoa, all of which are quite substantial and full-flavoured.

Rice

I use almost exclusively brown and white basmati rice in the majority of my cooking. These can be bought in large quantities and stored in an air-tight container. Other rice that I use would be risotto rice and pudding rice, which are usually bought in 500g packs. Basmati rice is better when washed thoroughly several times in cold water to remove the starch. Do this by soaking the rice in cold water for about twenty minutes before rinsing it in a strainer.

Lentils and Pulses

I keep a small stock of dried lentils and pulses in supply. Beans should all be soaked overnight and then cooked according to packet instructions (you can also follow the recipes in this book). Unfortunately, dried beans aren't something you can decide to have on a whim. Lentils tend to be a bit easier to work with, as they usually require about 40 minutes in a pan of water. I use both red and green lentils, yellow split peas, mung beans, urid beans and black-eyed beans. Red kidney beans and chickpeas are also great when cooked from dried. Remember, when you are soaking them, that they swell in the water. You will need to cover them in water to over an inch or so, so that they are still covered the next day.

Canned varieties of beans are available at all supermarkets. Chickpeas, red kidney beans, cannellini beans, borlotti and haricot beans are all easy to get hold of, pre-cooked and ready to use. If you're getting into aquafaba, then canned chickpeas are essential if you don't want to make the water yourself. Lentils are also available this way, sometimes in cartons, which you will find alongside the beans.

Grains

I've kept rice and grains separate for ease of reading and to keep things in general order of popularity. Other than rice, I only use a few grains in my cooking. These are: quinoa, bulgur wheat, oats, pearl barley and couscous. Quinoa is cooked similar to rice. Wash it in a few changes of cold water to remove the bitterness and then boil it for about 15-20 minutes, until all the water is absorbed. Couscous and bulgur wheat are the same in their cooking methods. Just pour boiling water over them, cover and leave to absorb. Oats can be cooked in a few ways: boiled or microwaved, as in with porridge, or oven baked as in with crumbles and flapjacks. You can also roast them with some oil and maple syrup to make your own granola (recipe page 77)

Spices

Spices can be bought whole or ready-ground and there are reasons for using both. I use ground spices most often for convenience, but there are plenty of occasions where toasted whole spices add a deep and robust flavour to a dish. Grinding you own is the best way to get the most flavour from your spices, in the same way that grinding your own coffee beans helps get a better espresso. There are a select range of spices that I use over and over again and I've listed them here for you so that you can scan them easily.

- Cinnamon – whole and ground
- Nutmeg – whole and ground
- Cardamom – whole
- Cloves – whole
- Mixed spice – ground
- All spice – ground
- Ginger - ground
- Cumin – whole and ground
- Coriander seeds – whole and ground
- Turmeric – ground
- Paprika – ground
- Garam masala – ground
- Chilli – ground, whole and flaked
- Star anise – whole
- Chinese five-spice blend – ground
- Cajun seasoning – ground
- Various curry powder blends – ground

This represents most of what I use on a regular basis. You may see a spice or a blend that catches your eye while you're out shopping and I encourage you to pick it up. The only way to know what it does is to try it out.

Sauces

There are a number of bottled and jarred sauces that I keep in stock that can really help enhance sauces you make from scratch. You'll be amazed at what a dollop of wholegrain mustard or even a squirt of ketchup can do to add depth to your homemade sauce. Again, I've listed these here for your convenience:

- Tomato ketchup
- Barbeque sauce – sweet and spicy
- Mustard – English, Dijon and Wholegrain
- Yeast extract (I actually can't stand it on toast, but in certain sauces and marinades it's outstanding).
- Hoisin sauce
- Soy sauce – dark and light, the difference is not just colour
- Vegan Worcester sauce (also gluten free)
- Tamari – gluten-free soy sauce
- Various nut butters
- Vegan mayonnaise
- Sriracha – hot chilli sauce in a squeezy bottle, usually found in the world food section
- Chilli oil – basically dried chilli flakes slowly cooked in oil and salt
- Tabasco sauce
- Sweet chilli sauce

Any one of these, and indeed some in combination, turn a whole number of dishes into something special. Mostly a spoonful or two is all you need when one of your own concoctions needs a little something extra. Having this list to hand can save many a meal, and has done for me on numerous occasions

Oils and Vinegars

Olive oil is a must in any kitchen and is the oil of choice in most of the recipes in this book. I rarely use vegetable or sunflower oil, but that is simply personal choice. Sesame oil is great to have for stir-fries and some dressings, though it does have a very strong flavour and so is not suitable for all cooking. Walnut oil again is quite flavoursome and can add a nice touch to salads. For a more neutral oil groundnut is ideal, which is made from peanuts. Rapeseed is also quite flavourless. Coconut oil is something I use more of these days. You can get the extra virgin coconut oil in 500g jars from a lot of stores and the price can vary considerably. It is solid when cold and does have an apparent coconut flavour, so it is not suitable for all cooking. It is wonderful for Indian food, however, and I also use it for pancakes and roast potatoes. Hemp oil has a lot of flavour but should be used sparingly as it can easily overpower a dish.

White wine and cider vinegars are two varieties I keep in constant supply. White wine vinegar is a little sweeter and is a good all-rounder for salad dressings. Cider vinegar is great for oriental dishes, or when you want to add a little sharpness to a dish. Balsamic is the Rolls Royce of vinegars, and I make sure I am never out of it. One of the finest and most simplistic salad dressings is extra virgin olive oil mixed with balsamic vinegar. It simply doesn't need anything else. Don't be tempted to buy a cheap balsamic, go for at least a mid-priced one. The cheap ones are harsh and not worth your time.

Fresh Fruit and Vegetables

This, of course, is the essence of vegan cooking. A ready supply of fresh fruit and veg from all over the world eaten on a daily basis. Tempting as it is to cram your fridge to bursting point with these delicious items, I must advise at least some caution. Fresh produce doesn't last long at all, so if you want to minimise your waste, minimise your supply. Try to predict your weekly needs before shopping for goods with a short use-by date. Some vegetables last longer than others. Avocados, apples and pears will keep for a while in your fridge, whereas spinach and salad leaves will only last days. Asparagus tips tend to go soft and mushy far quicker than you would like them to and raspberries are best eaten on the day you buy them. We are all busy people and we all buy plenty of things with good intentions, only to throw them out a week or so later.

You may already have a number of these items in your store cupboard. The rest you can gather over time and as you go through the recipes in this book. As with the fresh produce, my advice is to stay frugal at the start. It won't be long before your cupboards are stocked to the gills if you are doing serious cooking.

Cooking Techniques

Now that you've got your cupboards and fridge stocked up, we can look at some basic cooking techniques. It is good to get to grips with a variety of cooking methods to help improve your overall skills. I firmly believe that a good grounding in the basics is the key to successful cooking, particularly when it comes to taking it beyond the recipe-reading stage. This is the carry-water-chop-wood section of the book if you will.

Knife Care and Maintenance

Knives are the basic tool of cooking and food preparation, and it is important to keep them clean and sharp. They can also, as I'm sure you are aware, be a little dangerous, so it's also important to respect them. You do not need a huge array of knives to be a good cook. I have five that I use for just about everything:

•   A paring knife – A small-bladed knife used for little jobs like peeling, topping and tailing veg etc.
•   2 general cook's knives - These blades are between 6-8 inches long and are used for chopping, dicing, slicing, shredding and most general food preparation needs.
•   Carving knife - This is a longer and thinner knife, typically used in the slicing of meats. For our purposes it is good for slicing larger items such as pies and cakes.
•   A serrated knife – A long knife with a serrated edge, particularly useful when it comes to cutting bread.

Knife Sharpening

Maintaining your knife's edge is vital not only for accurate food cutting, but also for safety. A dull knife is prone to slipping, as more force is required to use it to do the same job as a sharp blade. There are two tools used for sharpening knifes: the steel and the carbon stone.

The stone has a rough surface and is useful for bringing back a very dull edge. Lay the stone on a flat surface (placing a tea towel underneath will stop it from slipping) and slide the blade, from the tip to the base, at a 30° - 40° angle away from you. Flip the knife over so that the back of the knife is facing you and draw the knife from the base to the tip at the same angle towards you. Repeat this action several times until your edge had returned.

There are a variety of steels available, but I would personally recommend only one, and that is the diamond steel. They range in price from £20-£40 or so, but they are worth the investment. A cheap steel will do little to keep your knife sharp and only cause you more frustration in the long run. Operating a steel takes a little practice, so start slowly and you'll get the technique soon enough. Begin at the tip of the steel with the base of the blade and the sharp edge pointing towards you. Draw downwards at the same 30° - 40° angle, so that you finish at the base of the steel with the tip of the blade. Switch to the other side of the blade and begin with the tip of the knife at the base of the steel. This time draw upwards away from you and finish with the base of the blade at the tip of the steel. Repeat these actions several times, until your knife edge has returned.

Purchasing and Storage

Knifes are best kept in a knife block, both for safety and convenience. They can be bought separately or as part of a set. Once again investment is crucial here. Cheap knives have poor-quality handles and have typically far too wide a blade to be of use, particularly with firmer vegetables like potatoes and squashes. Yet there is no need to pay hundreds. I paid between £20 and £35 per knife for my set and I have never been disappointed. Look for a thin and smooth blade and a good, forged handle.

Cooking Techniques

There are numerous techniques associated with good cooking. In this section we will cover the basics that you will be using throughout this book, from boiling and steaming to deep-frying and oven baking.

Boiling

Boiling is the process of submerging food and cooking it in water (or stock) that has been brought to boiling point. Food can be cooked either by submerging it in boiling water, or putting the food into cold water and boiling it from there. There are reasons to do both. Food brought to the boil from cold is less likely to be damaged than it would by placing it in already boiling water. It also helps to make the food tender, such as with potatoes. Certain foods are best put into the water after it has come to the boil, particularly those that take less time to cook. Pasta and less-hardy veg like broccoli, turn out soft and mushy if you try to boil them from cold water. Nutrients are also extracted in this way, which means you won't just lose colour and texture from those delicate vegetables.

Poaching

Poaching is when the food is cooked at a very low simmer in liquid deep enough to cover the food item. Often, after the poaching is done, the remaining liquid can be reduced and used to make a sauce for that food. Most things traditionally poached don't appear in the vegan diet, but pears and other fruits are a great example of how the vegan can take advantage of the poaching method.

Steaming

By far the healthiest method of cooking vegetables is steaming. Steaming is placing the food into the steam produced by the boiling water rather than the water itself. Many saucepan sets come with a steaming rack that sits on top of the main pan, and the lid is then placed on top of that. This traps the steam in the container where the food is placed.

This method cooks food quickly and evenly. It also helps keep nutrients locked in the food and helps them retain their colour. A whole number of vegetables can be steamed for around five minutes to provide optimum nutritional value.

Pan-Frying and Sautéing.

These are the method of cooking food in a shallow pan with some oil. Shallow frying will typically have more oil in the pan and is a way to get a crispy outer coating to the food. Sautéing generally requires about a tablespoon of oil and is used to seal the edges of food, or to brown them. For example; sautéed potatoes will usually be parboiled first so that they are tender after they have been sautéed.

Stir Frying

Whole or cut small vegetables can be stir fried in a small amount of oil to keep them crisp, colourful and to lock in goodness. Sesame or groundnut oil are great for stir fries, though vegetable or olive are also good. A wok is by far the best pan in which to stir fry food, due to its size and round shape. Don't over fill your pan when cooking like this, or you risk losing the crispness due to the build-up of steam and lengthier cooking times.

Roasting

The process of cooking in a large pan in the oven with a good quantity of oil. A slightly lesser amount of oil should be used than in shallow frying, though there should be enough to produce a crispy outer coating to the food. A high eat is used during roasting to seal the outside and lock in flavour.

Braising

This is a gentle method of cooking food involving a shallow pan, a lid, and a small amount of liquid. The food is cooked slowly, often after sautéing, and a lid kept on top to prevent moisture escaping. Only a small amount of liquid is required for vegetables due to the short cooking time and the releasing of the vegetables' own liquid.

Baking

This method involves once again cooking in the oven, but with a dry heat. The most common baked foods are breads and cakes. A little steam can be added during the baking process by using a spray-gun to spray small amounts of water vapour during cooking. This helps prevent too hard a crust from forming.

Grilling

Over hot coals, on a griddle pan or in the grill part of the oven, grilling is a way of fast cooking to seal or toast the outside of the food while leaving the centre relatively untouched. Peppers, aubergines, onions and asparagus are ideal vegetables to cook in this manner, as long as a little oil is added beforehand. Grills are also used for toasting and browning the top of food in order to finish it off.

Deep Frying

As we have become more health-conscious, our appetite for this cooking method has reduced. Deep frying is the total emersion of food in hot oil to cook it. Potato chips are the most popular food for deep frying, and a variety of vegetables can be coated in batter to protect them from the intense heat during frying, leaving the inside moist and tender. Air-fryers are becoming more popular as people shift away from high fat methods of cooking.

Useful Pans and Utensils

Different pans are better at different types of cooking, so it is ideal to make sure you have more than just the one. You should look to have at least two different sizes of saucepan: large and small. A few sizes in between would also be beneficial but not as essential. A non-stick frying pan is a must for a lot of the recipes in this book. I use a non-stick wok for a lot of my cooking, which allows me to start by sautéing and then add a sauce without changing pans.

Baking trays are used in this book for almost all baking and roasting. Try to have at least one, although having a couple to hand certainly couldn't hurt. Deeper oven dishes are good for things like lasagne and pasta bakes, and you can get shallow, circular trays with holes in that are designed for pizzas. Pizza trays aren't crucial. I went for many years without them, so no need to rush out and get one now.

Plastic and metal spatulas, wooden spoons, a potato masher, a good can opener (which, in my experience, has been surprisingly hard to find), a vegetable peeler (again, same problem) and a whisk are all going to get you out of trouble in the kitchen. A good quality blender is used in a lot of the recipes here, as is an electric whisk. You will also need a couple of decent mixing bowls, some weighing scales (ideally digital), measuring cups, jugs and spoons.

Greaseproof paper and tin foil are also needed. I try not to use cling film so much these days, but it does appear in this book a little. If you have a more environmentally-friendly option, then use that.

Cooking Basics

Before we dive into the recipes it would be good to go over a couple of basic cooking tips to get the most out of your time in the kitchen.

Get Organised

Planning ahead can make a world of difference when it comes to cooking, especially when it involves several courses or larger numbers of dinner guests. If you're new to cooking, then it's better to have all your steps laid out for you. Read all recipes from beginning to end before doing anything, and make sure you have the right equipment and ingredients to get the job done. If you are cooking for dinner guests, remember that *you* are a dinner guest too. If you are making at least two courses, you must allow time to eat with your party. They will feel guilty about sitting down and eating the main course while you're struggling to get the dessert into those new glasses you bought.

Taste Everything

You are the last stop between your food and the people you're feeding. As soon as it's cooked enough to taste it, then taste it. If you add more seasoning, taste it. If you pour in some cream or reduce a sauce, taste it. Don't let anything go out until you know that it's good enough.

Clean as You Go

There's nothing more likely to send pans flying angrily across the room than having nowhere to serve your food up, because your counter top is full of dirty pans and utensils. I nearly always cook with a sink full of hot, soapy water at the ready. If I'm waiting for water to boil, or if something is cooking in the oven, then I get to cleaning. I say nearly always, because I'm no saint. This, obviously, is much easier if you have a little helper in the kitchen. If you don't, then keep washing those dishes.

Make Sure You're Having Fun

Cooking can be hard work and stressful, especially when everything is coming together at the end. It's easy to let the pressure get to you and forget that the reason you're going to all this effort instead of just ordering a pizza is because you enjoy it. Cooking is creative, fun and extremely satisfying. So what if everyone has to wait an extra twenty minutes because your potatoes aren't cooked yet?

It's Okay, It's Vegan, Right?
A Few Notes on Healthy Eating

It's been a long day. Work, the commute, the kids have kicked your butt throughout most of it, and there' still dinner to do. Through the continuing chaos you pull open the freezer door and yank out various drawers and compartments. There is only one thing on your mind: What's the quickest and easiest thing I can cook that will keep everybody happy?

Boxes of easy-cooking delights stare back up at you. Sausages, pies, fishless fingers, potato wedges and a whole host of other goodies, just begging to be thrown into the oven on gas 6 for 20-30 minutes, while you reverse summersault from 20 metres into the nearest bottle of red wine. It is a buffet of post-traumatic relief.

Sound familiar?

I know it does to me. I can't count the number of nights I've come home from work, exhausted and detesting the thought of having to cook, but having to cook anyway. The simplest solution is always to fill a baking tray with pre-made, attractively-packaged, food, put it in the oven and wait. I've done it time without number.

What? You can be vegan and unhealthy?

For all of us who thought that living on a plant-based diet would peel off the pounds and turn us into supermodels, only to find out the hard way that that's not how it works, the answer is most definitely yes. Fat, salt and sugar are just as rife in vegan food as they are in everything else, and it is incredibly easy to over-indulge. Since discovering dairy-free ice cream I haven't been able to stop myself from eating it, and the it's okay, it's vegan excuse only stretches so far.

Tiredness, laziness and cravings are our biggest reasons for eating badly.

We all live busy lives, holding down jobs and running families. We have hospital visits, school appointments, taking the dog to the vet, not to mention squeezing in time to visit family and friends. It's no wonder we feel that we don't have time to cook. In our efforts to keep everything ticking over smoothly, we often neglect the one area of our lives that keeps us strong and healthy enough to manage everything else: maintaining a balanced and healthy diet. Doing so isn't easy, but it can be made just a little easier.

The average oven-ready meal takes 20-30 minutes to cook. In less than that time you can put a cup of brown basmati rice into a microwaveable bowl, put in two cups of water, a plate on top and cook your rice on 80% power. It takes about 17 minutes and doesn't need watching. While you're doing that, you can stir fry a couple of veggies in a wok, mix in a little tofu (Cauldron do a pre-cut, ready to stir fry variety), add some garlic paste from a jar and pour over some tamari and hoisin sauce. A healthy meal with minimal time and effort. Can't be bothered chopping veg? Supermarkets now stock a whole variety of vegetables that are ready cut, that you can rinse off and pour straight into a pan. You can get frozen diced and sliced onions. Mediterranean vegetables also come ready cut and frozen for your convenience. Try cooking those with some garlic, tomato puree, a can of chopped tomatoes, a little sea salt and serving with whole wheat pasta. A company called Zest do an amazing vegan pesto, which is a permanent feature in our store cupboard. Try putting a spoonful of that in with your med veg and tomato sauce for an instant Italian seasoning.

There are other ways to save time during the working week to allow for healthier eating. When I'm cooking things like pasta and rice, or one pot meals, I often cook enough for two days, so that I have less to do later in the week. Pre-cooked pasta and rice will last 3-4 days in the fridge and you can make the simplest of dishes with the leftovers. Try sautéing some green beans with olive oil and a little garlic, and then adding the pasta to that. Food doesn't always have to involve lots of ingredients but do try to cook at least one vegetable with every meal. That way, even if you haven't done much in the way of cooking, you're still getting essential nutrients.

If you have freezer space, one pot and oven dish meals can be made at the weekend and frozen for later consumption. I've included a few in this book to get you going. If you are cooking this way, freeze the food as soon as it has cooled down. Bacteria can build up if you leave your soup in the pan all day and store it away just before bedtime.

In the warmer weather, salads are a great way of cramming tons of veggie nutrition into a single meal. Bodybuilders have raw salads regularly with their meals to ensure they are getting the right amount of nutrition in their diets. They're like a vitamin bomb that doesn't leave you feeling bloated and miserable. Unfortunately, salads only last a day or so in the fridge, but they are quick and easy to assemble. Make sure you include plenty of grated raw ingredients in them, like carrot and beetroot. Also, make use of baby spinach and shredded raw kale instead of things like iceberg lettuce, which has a much lower nutritional value. Nuts and seeds are a wonderful addition to any salad, as is avocado and dried fruit. Play about and have fun with them. A word of caution: if you are storing salad for a day or two, then leave the dressing off until you are ready to serve. The dressing will wilt the salad in no time and leave you with a sloppy mess for dinner.

Fibre intake is extremely important and is one nutrient that is very easy to overlook in our day-to-day lives. Fibre not only keeps us regular, but also aids in reducing cholesterol levels in our bodies. Good sources of fibre are wholegrains, leafy greens, nuts and seeds, as well as oats. It is also in most fruits and vegetables, particularly if you leave the skins on. Flaxseeds and chia seeds are very good for fibre intake, so it is worth adding these whenever you can. The majority of recipes in this book contain whole wheat pasta or rice, and I have tried to include whole wheat flour in a number of ingredients where possible. Fibre, in my opinion should be a daily mission, as it is rather lacking in the processed foods we all eat too much of.

I firmly believe that the secret of healthy eating lies in consuming a variety of foods on a regular basis, with as few processed foods as possible. That being said, I am fully aware that we don't always have the time, or the inclination, to make everything from scratch, and therefore some processed foods are inevitable. Perhaps all we can do is try our best to keep them to a minimum.

THE RECIPES

COOKING THE ESSENTIALS

In this chapter we cover cooking the food that you will be using over and over again. The beans, the pulses, the rice, the pasta. All the regular items that make up the bulk of your dishes. You can refer back to these pages throughout you use of this book, and indeed throughout your cooking life. The recipes you find here will be at the heart of your cooking. Learn these over time and your cooking will come on in leaps and bounds.

DRIED RED KIDNEY BEANS

Ingredients:

1 cup dried kidney beans.
Enough cold water for soaking and cooking.

Makes 350g cooked beans.

Put the beans in a container and cover with cold water. Allow about 2 inches of water over the top of the beans as they will expand during soaking. Cover with a lid and soak for 12 hours, or overnight. Once soaked, drain the water and wash the beans in more cold water, then put them in a saucepan and fill with more water until you are about 3 inches over the beans. Bring to the boil and rapid boil the beans for 15 minutes. During this time, skin any foam off the top of the water with a spoon or ladle. Turn down the heat, cover with a lid, and simmer for 50 minutes, or until the beans are tender. Drain and either serve or chill for later use.

DRIED BLACK-EYED BEANS

Ingredients:

1 cup dried black-eyed beans
Enough cold water for soaking and cooking.

Make 400g cooked beans.

Put the beans in a container and cover with cold water. Allow about 2 inches of water over the top of the beans as they will expand during soaking. Cover with a lid and soak for 12 hours, or overnight. Once soaked, drain the water and wash the beans in more cold water, then put them in a saucepan and fill with more water until you are about 3 inches over the beans. Bring to the boil and rapid boil the beans for 15 minutes. During this time, skin any foam off the top of the water with a spoon or ladle. Turn down the heat, cover with a lid, and simmer for 1 hour, or until the beans are tender. Drain and either serve or chill for later use.

DRIED MUNG BEANS

Ingredients:

1 cup dried mung beans.
Enough water for soaking and cooking.

Makes about 500g cooked beans.

Put the beans in a container and cover with cold water. Allow about 2 inches of water over the top of the beans as they will expand during soaking. Cover with a lid and soak for 12 hours, or overnight. Once soaked, drain the water and wash the beans in more cold water, then put them in a saucepan and fill with more water until you are about 3 inches over the beans. Bring to the boil and rapid boil the beans for 10 minutes. During this time, skin any foam off the top of the water with a spoon or ladle. Turn down the heat, cover with a lid, and simmer for 15 minutes, or until the beans are tender and beginning to fall apart. Drain and either serve or chill for later use.

WHOLEGRAIN BASMATI RICE

Ingredients:

1 cup (150g) wholegrain basmati rice
500ml cold water

Serves 2

Soak the rice for 30 minutes, then drain and wash it. Put the 500ml cold water in a saucepan and bring to the boil. Add the rice. This will drop the temperature of the water, so bring it back up to the boil again. Turn the heat down to a low simmer and put on a tight-fitting lid (I put a small tea towel over the saucepan and then the lid on top). Gently simmer for about 20 minutes. All of the water will be absorbed during this time. Turn off the heat and leave the rice to stand for 5 minutes, then fork it through.

GREEN PEA FUSILLI

Ingredients:

1 pack (250g) Gluten-free green pea fusilli pasta
Enough water for boiling

Serves 2

Bring enough water to more than cover the pasta to the boil. Put in the dried pasta and then bring the water back up to the boil. Simmer for 6-8 minutes, until the pasta is tender but still with some bite. Drain and wash in boiling water and serve immediately.

WHOLE WHEAT SHORTCRUST PASTRY

Ingredients:

250g whole wheat flour
125g vegan margarine
1/2 tsp salt
1 tbsp ground flaxseeds
4 tbsp dairy-free milk

Make enough to cover 1 pie tin.

Put all the ingredients, apart from the milk, into a large mixing bowl and crumble between your fingers until you have a fine breadcrumb texture. Pour in the milk and bring the dough together with your hands. Knead into a fine dough on a floured surface, then cover and chill in the fridge for at least 30 minutes before using.

DRIED WHOLE WHEAT SPAGHETTI

Ingredients:

500g dried whole wheat spaghetti
Enough water to boil

Serves 2

Fill a large saucepan two thirds of the way up with water and bring to the boil. Once it is boiling, twist the dried spaghetti slightly in your hand, so that when you release it into the pan it fans out around the edges. As it softens, push down the edges of the spaghetti that are still sticking out over the lip of the pan, then begin to gently stir with a fork. This helps separate the strands so that none clump together. Simmer for 10-12 minutes, stirring a couple of times to ensure the strands don't stick. Strain, wash in hot water from a kettle and serve. If serving at a later time, wash in cold water to stop the cooking process.

DRIED GREEN LENTILS

Ingredients:

1 cup dried green lentils, rinsed until the water runs clear

Enough water for boiling.

Makes about 400g cooked lentils.

Bring the water to the boil and add the lentils. Rapid boil them for 10 minutes, skimming off any foam that forms on top. Turn down the heat and simmer for 40 minutes, until tender.

DRIED PEARL BARLEY

Ingredients:

1 cup dried pearl barley, rinsed until the water runs clear

Enough water to cover about 2 inches over the barley.

Makes about 500g cooked pearl barley.

Bring the water to the boil and add the barley. Turn down the heat and simmer for 40 minutes, until tender. Skim off any foam that forms.

SWEET BUCKWHEAT SHORTCRUST PASTRY

GLUTEN-FREE

Prep time: 10 minutes. Chill time: 1 hour

Makes enough for 1 pie.

Ingredients:

450g buckwheat flour
½ tsp salt
1 ½ tsp baking powder
75g icing sugar
200g vegan margarine
150ml rice milk

This is a good standard sweet and gluten-free pastry that should take care of most of your sweet pie needs.

Method:

Put the flour, salt, baking powder and sugar into a mixing bowl and combine. Put the margarine in in separate little chunks, then use your fingers to work the margarine through, using the rubbing technique, until it resembles fine bread-crumbs.

Pour in the rice milk and use a table knife to mix it in. Bring it all together using your hands and form into a ball. Wrap in clingfilm and chill or an hour before using.

Sauces & Dressings

Coriander, Lime and Hazelnut Dressing

Gluten-free

Prep time: 5-10 minutes, plus a couple of second in the blender.

Makes about 400ml.

Ingredients:

50g fresh coriander
2 cloves garlic, bashed with the flat of a knife
30g hazelnuts
Juice of 1 lime
1 tsp Dijon mustard
2 tbsp maple syrup
75ml cider vinegar
350ml olive oil
Salt and black pepper to taste.

This dressing is an ideal way of using up leftover bunches of coriander, which tend to wilt quite quickly. It's good with potato salad, or with my falafel recipe (page 193). Light and refreshing, with a good hint of garlic and lime, it will serve very well on a whole number of spicy dishes.

Method:

Put all the ingredients into a blender and pulse for a few seconds at a time, until you have a smooth consistency. Chill until ready to serve.

Vegan Cheese Sauce

Prep time: 5 minutes. Cooking time: 10 minutes

Serves 2

Ingredients:

45g vegan margarine
2 tbsp gram flour
500ml dairy-free milk
1 vegan stock cube (also gluten free)
2 tbsp nutritional yeast
50g vegan cheese
1 tsp Dijon mustard.

Melt the margarine in a saucepan and add the gram flour. Mix to form a thick paste (it will thicken very quickly). Add the milk a little bit at a time, whisking continuously, to create a thick white sauce. Whisk out any lumps each time you add some milk before adding any more. Bring to a gentle simmer and add the stock cube, nutritional yeast, vegan cheese and mustard. Whisk again and simmer for about 4 minutes, until you have a smooth, thick and yellow sauce.

Masala Sauce

Prep Time: 5 minutes. Cooking time: 15 minutes.

Serves 2

Ingredients:

2 tbsp coconut oil
½ onion, very finely diced
1 clove garlic, minced
6 cherry tomatoes, chopped
2 tsp turmeric
1 tsp ground cumin
1 tsp ground coriander
3 tsp tandoori masala curry powder
2 tbsp tomato puree
2 tbsp dairy-free yoghurt
½ tsp salt
100ml cold water
200ml vegan cream
1 ½ tbsp brown sugar

Heat the coconut oil in a saucepan. Fry the onions for 2 minutes, then add the garlic and fry for one more minute, stirring often. Add the cherry tomatoes and cook for 2 minutes, then add the spices, tomato puree, yoghurt and salt. Mix well and cook until it starts to bubble. Pour in the cold water and bring to the boil. Simmer for 3 minutes, then pour in the cream and brown sugar. Simmer gently for 3-4 more minutes, until you have a thick sauce. You can either serve as it is or blend first with a hand blender to create a smoother sauce.

SUMMER BERRY COMPOTE

Cooking time: 25 minutes.
Cooling time: about 90 minutes.

Makes 1 medium jar.

Ingredients:

1 x 500g pack frozen summer berries
200g unrefined sugar
1 tsp vanilla extract.

This is a very quick and delicious compote that you can make out of a packet of frozen berries from the supermarket. It takes about 25 minutes, plus about an hour or so of chilling time (that is if you want it chilled, because you can also have it warm). It goes with a variety of things. Try it with granola and yoghurt (page 84), or with my whole wheat apple crumble (page 247). You can also spread it on toast, or simply spoon it into your mouth! It'll keep in the fridge for a few weeks, so you can enjoy it any time.

Method

Put all the ingredients into a saucepan and bring to the boil, stirring occasionally. You will not need any additional liquid as plenty will come from the berries. Simmer gently for about 25 minutes, until the compote is thick and easily coats the back of a spoon. Turn off the heat and allow to cool fully before storing in the fridge.

VEGAN 'HONEY' & ORANGE DRESSING

Prep time: 5 minutes.

Makes about 175ml

Ingredients:

50ml olive oil
Juice of 1 orange
35ml white wine vinegar
3 tbsp coconut nectar
Pinch salt

Coconut nectar makes a great substitute for honey and is perfect for this dressing.

Method

Combine all the ingredients together into a bowl and whisk thoroughly. Serve chilled.

MARINARA SAUCE

Prep time: 15 minutes.
Cooking time: up to 1 hour.

Make 1.5 litres (6 servings)

Ingredients:

4 tbsp olive oil
1.8kg fresh, ripe vine tomatoes, roughly chopped
6 cloves fresh garlic, chopped
1 tube tomato puree
1 ½ tsp sea salt
25g fresh parsley leaves, finely chopped.

Good marinara sauce comes from good, ripe, fresh tomatoes. It doesn't come from canned tomatoes. You can, of course, make it from canned tomatoes, but it will not be as good as if you chop up your own fresh produce and cook it from scratch. Fresh, ripe, tomatoes produce a sweet and rich sauce. I get mine from a local market, as the ones in the supermarket are never ripe, and therefore will not produce the same sweetness. The absolute best way is to grow your own and pick them at the perfect time. Straight from your garden to the pan! That's not possible for everyone, of course, so your local market is the best bet. It's the same with the garlic. Use the freshest cloves you can. If yours has been hanging around for a couple of weeks, then get yourself a new one for this dish. Trust me, you'll be glad you did.

This recipe makes about a litre and a half, which will serve 6 people. If you're cooking for two, then go ahead and make the full batch, then just freeze it into separate portions. Consider this your basic Italian tomato sauce. If you're feeling lazy one evening, just serving this with some spaghetti and grated vegan parmesan is a perfect and simple evening meal. Other times you can add things to it for a deeper and richer flavour.

Method

Heat the oil in a large saucepan. Turn the heat down and add the garlic. Cook it gently for 2-3 minutes, so that the flavour of the garlic infuses with the oil, but that the garlic does not burn. Add half of the chopped tomatoes and cook for another three minutes, stirring occasionally. Once the tomatoes have softened a little then add the rest of them and bring the whole lot to the boil. Add the tomato puree, sea salt and parsley and simmer gently with no lid for about 40 minutes, stirring from time to time to make sure the sauce doesn't stick. The sauce should have reduced by about a third at this point. Taste for seasoning and add more if necessary.

From here you can either serve it as it is, or puree it if you want a smooth sauce. If you are saving it for another time, then allow it to cool fully before portioning it out and either chilling or freezing it.

GRAPE AND BALSAMIC VINEGAR DRESSING

GLUTEN-FREE

Prep time: 5 minutes.

Makes about 175ml.

Ingredients:

100g seedless red grapes
50ml olive oil
3 tbsp balsamic vinegar
¼ tsp harissa paste
¼ tsp wholegrain mustard
2 tbsp maple syrup

Put all the ingredients into a blender and puree until smooth. You can either strain out the grape skin using a sieve, or keep it in.

PLUM SAUCE

GLUTEN-FREE

Prep time: 10 minutes. Cooking time: 25 minutes.

Makes 500ml.

Ingredients:

1 tbsp sesame oil
½ small onion, finely diced
1 large clove garlic, chopped
350g plums, halved, stoned and cut into wedges
100g sugar
200ml veg stock (gluten-free)
2 tbsp cider vinegar
½ tsp chilli oil
2 tbsp tamari

Heat the oil in a small saucepan and fry the onions and garlic together for 2-3 minutes, stirring often. Add the plums and cook for another 3 minutes, then pour in the rest of the ingredients. Bring to the boil and simmer gently for 25 minutes, stirring from time to time, until you have a thick sauce. Allow the sauce to cool and then puree in a blender until smooth. Chill until ready to use.

'BLUE CHEESE' DRESSING

GLUTEN-FREE

Prep time: 5 minutes. Cooking time: 3 minutes.

Makes about 400g

Ingredients:

200g vegan mayonnaise
2 tbsp white wine vinegar
1 tsp garlic puree
1 tsp Dijon mustard
Juice of ½ lemon
50ml olive oil
Pinch of salt and black pepper
1 tbsp olive oil
75g vegan blue style cheese

Put all the ingredients, apart from the tablespoon of olive oil and the blue cheese, into a mixing bowl and whisk until fully combined.

Heat the tablespoon of olive oil in a small pan and add the blue cheese. Cook over a gently heat for about 3 minutes, until the cheese has melted, then add this to the dressing mixture. Whisk it in thoroughly, put the dressing into a container and chill until ready to use.

TZATZIKI

GLUTEN-FREE

Prep time: 4-5 minutes

Makes about 500g.

Ingredients:

½ cucumber
350g dairy-free yoghurt
1 ½ tsp garlic puree
1 tsp Dijon mustard
2 tbsp olive oil
Salt and black pepper to taste

Cut the cucumber in half lengthways. Use a teaspoon to remove the seeds and then grate both halves into a mixing bowl. Put the rest of the ingredients into the bowl with the cucumber and mix thoroughly with a large spoon.

Put into a container, cover and chill until ready to use. Will last about 3 days.

HOMEMADE VEGAN MAYONNAISE

Prep time: 10 minutes or so.

Makes about 250g

Ingredients:

125ml soya milk
1 tsp Dijon mustard
1 tsp lemon juice (a small squeeze will do fine)
Pinch sea salt
250ml sunflower oil

Making your own mayonnaise is extremely easy. All you need is five ingredients, a blender and a little bit of patience. Traditionally, mayonnaise is made by emulsifying oil with egg yolks. This is done very slowly, literally drop-by-drop at the beginning, to allow the two ingredients to bind together. Vegan mayo is made in the same way. The only difference is we trade egg yolks for soya milk. As long as you take your time adding the oil the results will be fantastic, and it tastes creamier than a lot of the shop-bought products.

Method:

Put all the ingredients, apart from the oil, into a blender and start to blend. While the blender is on pour the oil, at first a drop at a time, into the spout to mix with the rest of the ingredients. Slowly build up to a tiny stream of oil after a while. You can rest your blender periodically if you need to, just remember to start it up again before you begin pouring.

Continue this until all the oil is gone. By the end you will have a thick mayonnaise. Empty into a container and keep refrigerated.

MANGO CHUTNEY

Prep time: 10 minutes.
Cooking time: 45 minutes.
Chilling time: at least 2 hours.

Makes 500ml.

Ingredients:

1 tbsp rapeseed oil
1 medium onion, finely diced
1 tsp garlic puree
1 ½ tsp ginger puree
2 ripe mangoes, peeled and diced
100ml cold water
½ tsp turmeric powder
½ tsp cumin powder
¼ tsp chilli powder
150g unrefined sugar
Small handful coriander leaves, chopped

I've always preferred a homemade mango chutney to anything bought in the shops. I find that the stuff that comes in jars generally just tastes of sugar and not much else. If you make it yourself, you can taste the ingredients. You can taste the sweetness, sure, but you've also got the flavours of the fruit and spices. That's how it should be. It's very important that you have ripe mangoes for this dish. Unripe fruit will not cook down and will be bitter instead of sweet. When you're buying them, just make sure that you are able to squeeze them slightly.

Try this recipe the next time you're planning an Indian meal and you'll be pleasantly surprised by the difference.

Method:

Heat the oil in a small saucepan and gently fry the onions for 4-5 minutes. You don't want them to burn as this will taint the dish. Add the garlic and ginger and fry for a minute more. Put in the mangoes, then add all the other ingredients.

Bring it to the boil, turn the heat down to a simmer and put a lid on the pan. Simmer for 25 minutes with the lid on the pan, then take it off and simmer for another 15 minutes. You will need to stir more as it cooks down to prevent it from sticking.

Turn off the heat and allow the chutney to cool. At this point you can either keep it chunky, or blend it until mostly smooth, depending on how you like it. Place the chutney in a container with a lid and chill for at least 2 hours before serving.

BEST VEGAN GRAVY

GLUTEN-FREE

Prep time: 10 minutes.
Cooking time: 35-45 minutes.

Serves 6-8.

Ingredients:

2 tbsp rapeseed oil
(groundnut is also fine)
1 medium onion, large
diced
2 celery sticks (including
leaves if you have them),
sliced
1 medium carrot, skin left
on, washed and sliced
2 cloves garlic, smashed
2 med tomatoes, cut into
wedges
3-4 tbsp buckwheat flour,
depending on how thick
you want the gravy
1 litre potato water
500ml tap water
2 veg stock cubes (gluten-free)
1 tbsp yeast extract
2 tbsp tamari (gluten-free)
1 tbsp Dijon mustard

I first learned to do vegetarian gravy properly long before I gave up eating meat. It was a huge eye-opener for me. The knowledge that you could make really good gravy without using meat stock went against everything I'd been brought up to believe. At that point it was my job to make the gravy, so I was doing it often and learned to do it well. I took that knowledge with me and, like with most things, I adapted it over time. The gravy I make now is a little different from that one and has, as such, developed its own unique character. You can use all regular water if that's what you have, but I would recommend using the leftover water from boiled potatoes for two thirds of your liquid. It makes a big difference to the flavour. I urge you to try this gravy with your next Sunday roast. I promise it will be a crowd-pleaser.

Method:

Heat the oil in a large saucepan and fry the onion, celery and carrots for 5 minutes, stirring often. Add the garlic and fry for 2 minutes more, then add the tomatoes. Cook for 4-5 more minutes, until the tomatoes are soft.

Put in the buckwheat flour and stir to fully combine. This will give you a sort of thick, vegetable goo, but that's how it's supposed to be. Now add a little bit of your potato water and stir in rapidly. It will start to thicken immediately. Add a bit more and stir again. In the beginning it will be quite thick, but it will thin out as more water goes into the pot. The important thing is to fully amalgamate the sauce before adding any more water, so that you don't end up with lumps.

When all the potato water is in you can then add the tap water and the rest of the ingredients. Bring the sauce to the boil, stirring from time to time, and then turn down the heat and simmer, without a lid, for 35-45 minutes. The gravy will reduce by about a third during this time and the sauce will become rich and smooth.

After this time taste it to see if it needs any more seasoning and add some salt and pepper if needed (I never do for this gravy). Turn off the heat and allow to stand for about 10 minutes.

Take a jug or container with at least a litre volume and stand a sieve over it. Pass the gravy through the sieve a ladleful at a time, which will remove all the vegetables and leave you with a smooth gravy. Discard the vegetables and serve the gravy when ready.

BREAKFAST

GRANOLA WITH SPICED APPLES AND BLUEBERRIES.

Prep time: 10 minutes.
Cooking time: 15 minutes.
Cooling time: 5 minutes.

Serves 2

Ingredients:

For the spiced apples:
Two medium apples,
cored, peeled and cut into
wedges
1 tsp coconut oil
½ tsp cinnamon
¼ tsp allspice
¼ tsp grated nutmeg
2 tbsp coconut nectar
(brown sugar will also do
fine)
1 tbsp cold water

For the rest:
150g simple granola
(homemade or bought)
6 tbsp plain dairy-free
yoghurt
2 handfuls fresh blueberries

Here is a stunning and simplistic contrast of hot and cold. The apples are served warm and really stand out against the chilled yoghurt and blueberries. Use gluten-free granola to make it gluten-free.

Method:

Heat the coconut oil in a pan and gently cook the apples for 10 minutes until soft and slightly browned. Add the spices and cook for another 2 minutes, then add the coconut nectar and water and cook for a further 3-4 minutes. Allow the apples to cool for 5 minutes before serving.

Split the granola into two bowls, then put 3 tbsp of the yoghurt on top of each serving. Spoon half of the spiced apples onto each helping of yoghurt and then put a handful of blueberries on top of that. If the granola is too dry for your taste you can always add some dairy-free milk to the dish.

TOFU SCRAMBLE WITH RED ONION, MUSHROOM & ROSEMARY

GLUTEN-FREE

Prep time: 15 minutes.
Cooking time: 10-15 minutes.

Serves 3-4

Ingredients:

1 x 400g pack plain tofu in water
50g gram flour
100ml cold water
2 tbsp olive oil
½ red onion, thinly sliced
6-8 chestnut mushrooms, sliced
1 sprig rosemary, roughly chopped
2 cloves garlic, chopped
2 tbsp nutritional yeast
50ml dairy-free cream (coconut cream is fine if not available)
Salt and pepper to taste

The first recipe I came across for tofu scramble didn't quite sit well with me. It used turmeric to get the colour and as a result it was a little too spicy. It was also rather dry and didn't really have a texture that was close to what I was trying to achieve. I experimented over time until I came up with this recipe, which I believe replicates scrambled egg quite well. The trick, I've discovered, is to use a gram flour and water roux to get the desired colour and consistency. Soya cream is also added at the end just a minute or so before serving to enrich it even further. The dish dries up very quickly, so it is better to serve it straight away. If this isn't possible, a little dairy-free milk mixed in and reheated will get the right consistency back. The recipe itself is gluten free, you just have to serve it on the bread of your choice.

Method

First drain the tofu by placing it in a clean tea towel and putting a heavy saucepan on top of it. Set aside for 10 minutes. While that is draining put the gram flour into a mixing bowl and add the cold water, a little bit at a time, whisking constantly to prevent any lumps from forming.

Cut the drained tofu into small cubes and heat the oil in a non-stick pan. Fry the tofu for 5 minutes, until slightly browned on most sides. When this is done use a potato masher to break up the tofu pieces in the pan. You don't have to break them all up fine but rather get a good lumpy egg-like consistency. Add the onions, mushrooms and rosemary and cook for two more minutes, stirring occasionally. Once the mushrooms have wilted a little add the garlic and fry for another minute, then add the nutritional yeast and stir in. Pour over the gram flour and water mixture and stir in again. It will start to thick immediately. Cook for a minute or two and then add the cream to get the texture of fresh-cooked scrambled eggs. Season with the salt and pepper to taste and serve on your favourite bread.

Three Ways with Porridge

Porridge can be a bit of a breakfast staple for a lot of us, but it's easy to get stuck in a rut and have it the same way over and over again. With this in mind, I've come up with a few ideas that might broaden your horizons a little. They're all very easy to make, so do give them a try the next time you're in the mood for something different for breakfast. Use gluten-free oats if you need to.

GLUTEN-FREE

Porridge with Pumpkin Seeds, Almonds and Flaxseeds

Prep time: 5 minutes. Cooking time: 4-5 minutes.

Serves 2

Ingredients:

1 cup almond milk
1 cup water
1 cup porridge oats
3 tbsp maple syrup
20g sultanas
10g flaked almonds
10g pumpkin seeds
2 tbsp flaxseeds

Put the milk and water into a saucepan and bring to the boil, pour in the porridge oats and simmer for about 2 minutes, stirring continuously, until the porridge had thickened. Serve into two bowls, then pour half of the maple syrup onto each serving. Top the porridge with half each of the rest of the ingredients and serve immediately.

Overnight Oats with Raspberries

Prep time: 5 minutes. Chilling time: overnight.

Serves 1-2

Ingredients:
½ cup rolled oats
1 cup dairy-free milk
4 tbsp dairy-free vanilla yoghurt
1 tbsp chia seeds
3 tbsp maple syrup
60g raspberries, fresh or frozen

I'm a new convert to overnight oats, but now that I've had them I'm hooked. They are ridiculously simple to make and there's no cooking involved. Just put your ingredients into a tub, leave them in the fridge overnight and wake up to perfect oats for breakfast.

Method:

Put all the ingredients into a tub. Give it a good mix around with a spoon, then put the lid on the tub and store in the fridge overnight. Garnish in the morning with more raspberries and flaked almonds.

Nut Butter and Chocolate Porridge

GLUTEN-FREE

Prep time: 5 minutes.
Cooking time: 5 minutes.

Serves 1-2

Ingredients:

2 cups dairy-free milk
1 ½ tbsp nut butter
1 cup porridge oats
Pinch of salt
4 tbsp maple syrup
4-6 cubes dark, dairy-free chocolate

This porridge is simply delicious, and so decadent it's almost like a dessert for breakfast. You're better off making this one in a saucepan to allow the nut butter to melt and properly amalgamate. Use any nutter butter you like for this.

Method:

Heat the milk up in a pan and add the nut butter. Stir continuously to break up the butter and melt it into the milk. Add the oats, salt and maple syrup and simmer for 5 minutes, until the porridge has thickened.

Take off the heat and stir in the chocolate. Serve and garnish with some grated chocolate and nuts of your choice.

BANANA AND SULTANA PANCAKES

Prep time: 5 minutes. Cooking time: about 6-8 minutes per batch.

Makes about 15 pancakes.

Ingredients:

200g self-raising flour
1 tsp baking powder
50g unrefined sugar
½ tsp cinnamon
¼ tsp ground nutmeg
Pinch sea salt
300ml dairy-free milk
1 tsp vanilla extract
1 medium banana, mashed with a fork
60g sultanas
1 tbsp coconut nectar
Flavourless oil for frying.

Pancakes are a great way to start any day, but there's not always the time to make them. I usually do mine on the weekends, when everyone can enjoy them at their leisure. I have a preference for the thicker, American style pancakes. For these you need a much thicker batter, that you spoon onto your hot pan. They tend to naturally fall into the shape that you want, but you can always round them off a little by pushing the edges in with the tip of a spatula as they are cooking. You don't want to overcrowd the pan, as they will run into each other and you will have to separate them. My process is to keep a low oven running, cook the pancakes in batches of three, and keep the rest warm as I'm cooking more. This way you can also enjoy them with your family, instead of cooking them to order.

Method

Put the oven on a low heat.

Put the flour, baking powder, sugar, spices and salt into a large mixing bowl. Add the milk a little at a time, whisking constantly, until you have a smooth and thick batter. Add the rest of the ingredients, apart from the oil, and mix together.

Heat a tablespoon or so of the oil in a frying pan until it gets very hot. Spread it about the pan so that it covers the whole surface. Using a large dessert spoon, put three dollops of the pancake batter into the pan, leaving about an inch space between them. Make sure you get some sultanas on each spoonful, as they have a way of sinking to the bottom. They will start to spread out while they are cooking. Leave them to cook for 2-3 minutes. They are ready to turn when a lot of bubbles have formed on the top surface. Gently flip them over using a spatula and cook them for the same amount of time on the other side. When they are done, transfer them to a baking tray and keep warm in the oven while you cook the next batch. Repeat the process until you have used up all the batter.

PAN FRIED RED GRAPEFRUIT WITH CINNAMON SUGAR SYRUP

Cooking time: about 15 minutes.

Serves 2.

Ingredients:

1 tbsp coconut oil
1 red grapefruit, cut into 8 wedges
3 tbsp cinnamon sugar
50ml orange juice

I think grapefruit is a bit of a love it/hate it food. I grew up with my mother eating it. She would cut it in half and sprinkle sugar on the top, then eat it with a spoon. I remember trying it and getting the most bitter, sour taste in my mouth. I think it was a long time before I ate grapefruit again after that. The red ones are definitely more palatable, so if you're unsure about grapefruit, then that's a good place to start. I've used them here because they are sweeter and work well with the syrup. For lovers of the fruit, give this dish a whirl and see what you think.

Method:

Heat the oil in a frying pan and fry the grapefruit segments for about 4-5 minutes on each side, turning twice throughout, until they are starting to brown. Pour the sugar into the pan and then add the orange juice. Stir to mix in and then simmer for about 2-3 minutes, or until there is just a small amount of syrup left.

Serve 4 segments of fruit onto each plate and drizzle the syrup around the edge.

HOMEMADE GRANOLA

GLUTEN-FREE

Prep time: 5 minutes.
Cooking time: 30 minutes.

Makes about 300g.

Ingredients:

50ml groundnut oil
25ml sesame oil
50ml maple syrup
2tbsp coconut nectar
Pinch flaked sea salt
175g rolled oats

Making you own granola might seem like an unnecessarily bothersome thing to do, but it's actually ridiculously simple and requires minimum effort. All you do is mix some oil and sweetener together with a pinch of salt and then mix the oats into that. Put it in the oven for about half an hour and you're done. This recipe is for a basic version, as in just roasted rolled oats, but you can go anywhere from there.

Method

Preheat the oven to gas 4/180C/350F and line a baking tray with greaseproof paper.

Put all the ingredients, apart from the oats, into a mixing bowl and whisk together until fully incorporated. Add the oats and stir with a spoon again until fully mixed. Spread the mixture out onto the baking tray and place in the middle of the oven for 20 minutes. Take them out and give them a good mix around, then put them back in for another 10 minutes, or until golden brown. Allow to cool completely on the tray. You can store them in an air-tight container for about 6 weeks.

Try the same recipe as above, but this time add 25g pumpkin seeds, 50g rasins and 20g flaked almonds.

SPICED PUMPKIN FRENCH TOAST

I grew up with egg bread. It was a thing in my house. My sister and I would come downstairs after we had been put to bed, walking as quietly as possible to prevent our footfalls creaking on the stairs and ensuring our discovery. We knew we would be caught eventually, my father would still be awake and in the kitchen, but we didn't want to be caught on the staircase. It was far easier to be sent back to bed if you were only part-way through your journey. Once you were passed the lounge and into the kitchen… well, you were pretty much home free. No point sending us straight back up now. The smell of frying would become stronger as we passed the stairs and into the lounge, and the sound of the spatula scraping against the pan would be more audible to us now. Those sounds and smells would act as a current, drawing us nearer to their source.

We would hover in the kitchen doorway and watch my father at work at the stove. He was probably aware of our presence long before he let it be known to us, but for a good few minutes he would carry on as if we were not there. This routine was reiterated time and again: My father would look over at us, ask us what we were doing out of bed. Our response was inevitably coy silence and he would fill the gap by inquiring if we were hungry. We would nod in the affirmative. From that point on we would be allowed to sit on the kitchen counter while my father dipped sliced bread into a rather milky and always heavily peppered scrambled egg mixture. He would fry each slice individually in hot butter, turning it several times until the edges were well browned but the middle still soft and yellowed. Ours would be cut and served on little plates but he would not do this until all the cooking was done. There was seldom any informal eating of meals in my childhood. Each one was served at the dining table no matter how impromptu the occasion, and late-night stolen suppers were no exception. So, we would sit at the table with my father and eat the egg bread with quiet interest and, when that was done, he would take us back to bed.

GLUTEN-FREE

Prep time: 20 minutes, including pumpkin prep and cooking. Cooking time: About 15 minutes.

Serves 3-4

Ingredients:

300g diced pumpkin flesh, cooked and allowed to drain. (I put mine in a microwavable bowl with some water and a lid for 9 minutes on 80% power)
4 heaped tbsp gram flour
50g dark brown sugar
1 ½ tsp ground cinnamon
½ tsp ground nutmeg
¼ tsp ground mixed spice
½ tsp salt
Pinch cayenne pepper
300ml almond milk
100ml vegan cream
50g raisins
1 loaf of your chosen bread (I used date and walnut)
Coconut oil for frying.

I recall these memories almost every time I dip bread in some form of batter and fry it. These days I don't use egg for my mixtures but have found that there are an abundance of alternatives that actually taste a lot better. This one I've created to take advantage of the pumpkin season. It has that beautifully sweet and cinnamon flavour that suits the vegetable so well and makes quite a decadent breakfast or brunch for the weekend. You can also, as my father would do with his own version, have it as a late supper. The recipe itself is gluten-free but I have used a wheat artisan bread to dip into. All you have to do is change it to the bread of your choice.

Method:

Preheat the oven to Gas 2/150C/300F

Put the cooked and drained pumpkin flesh into a mixing bowl and add the gram flour. Mix these together to get rid of all the lumps. Add the sugar, spices and salt and mix again, then use a whisk and add the almond milk a little at a time, whisking as you go. Once you have added all of the milk, whisk in the cream and then stir in the raisins. Leave your batter to rest while you cut your chosen bread into about 8 thick slices.

Heat a teaspoon of coconut oil in a non-stick frying pan until very hot. Dip one slice of bread into the batter, making sure to catch some of the raisins. Let it drain off slightly and then add it to the frying pan. You may want to add some of the raisins from the mixture onto the top of the bread at this point if you didn't manage to scoop any up. Fry two slices of the battered bread at a time, for about 3 minutes each side, or until browned and crisp. Place the cooked bread on a baking tray and put in the oven to keep warm until all the batches are finished. Serve with extra raisins, autumn fruit of your choice and maple syrup.

BUCKWHEAT BLUEBERRY SQUARES

GLUTEN-FREE

Prep time: 10 minutes.
Cooking time: 25-30 minutes, plus cooling time.

Makes 12 squares.

Ingredients:

2 tbsp ground flaxseeds
50ml cold water

Dry:
350g buckwheat flour
2 tsp baking powder
1 tsp bicarbonate of soda
1 tsp xantham gum
1 tsp salt
250g unrefined sugar

Wet:
4 tbsp maple syrup
250g rice milk
1 tsp vanilla extract
65g vegan margarine
100ml vegetable oil
250g fresh blueberries

Consider this a cross between a blueberry muffin and a brownie. You can make them the night before to have a great treat for breakfast, without any fuss in the morning. Just like a brownie, you turn the tray upside down onto a board to empty the contents, but in this case the cake will be upside down, so my suggestion is to immediately put a cooling rack on top and flip it back the right way. It you don't do this the top will become soggy and stick to the board. I've used buckwheat flour to keep these gluten-free.

Method:

Mix the ground flaxseeds and water together in a small bowl and set aside for 10 minutes.

Preheat the oven to gas 6/200C/400F and line a rimmed baking tray with greaseproof paper.

Put all the dry ingredients into a large mixing bowl and mix together. Put in the flaxseeds and water mixture, then add the wet ingredients, apart from the blueberries and whisk together until you get a smooth batter. Fold in the blueberries at the end and pour the whole mixture into the baking tray. Smooth out the top with the back of a spoon and cook in the middle of the oven for 25-30 minutes, or until risen and brown.

Once it is cooked, allow to cool slightly for 5 minutes, then tip the tray upside down onto a suitably-sized surface (a large chopping board is good for this). Carefully remove the greaseproof paper and then put a rectangle cooking rack on top of the upside-down cake. Gently turn the whole lot over, including the chopping board to keep everything in place, then remove the board so that the whole cake can cool on the rack without gathering steam.

Once cool, cut into 12 squares and cover and chill until morning.

GRANOLA WITH YOGHURT & SUMMER BERRY COMPOTE

GLUTEN-FREE

Prep time: 2 minutes.

Serves 1

Ingredients:

4 tbsp homemade granola (see page 77)
2 tbsp summer berry compote (see page 52)
6 tbsp natural, dairy-free yoghurt.

This dish is simply a matter of putting together other recipes from the book and it makes for a delightful and quick breakfast if you have already made the other dishes. Use gluten-free oatsd where required.

Method:

To make the dish, simply spoon 2 tablespoons of granola into the bottom of a dish or glass, spoon 3 tablespoons of yoghurt on top of that. Top with a tablespoon of berry compote, and then repeat the process until you have two layers of each.

LUNCH

Sweet Pepper & Tomato Soup with Ciabatta Croutons and Basil Oil

EASY TO MAKE GLUTEN-FREE

Prep Time: 10 minutes. Cooking Time: 25 minutes.

Serves 4

Ingredients:

For the Soup:
1 small onion, diced
2 bell peppers, orange, red or yellow, deseeded and diced
2 cloves garlic, chopped
4 tbsp tomato puree
1 can chopped tomatoes
3 cans cold water
3 veg stock cubes (vegan and gluten-free)
100ml vegan cream
Salt and pepper to taste

For the Croutons:
1 large or 2 small ciabatta rolls
Pinch sea salt
½ tbsp dried oregano
3 tbsp olive oil

For the Basil Oil:
100ml olive oil
Large handful basil leaves
1 small garlic clove
Pinch of salt
Ground black pepper.

This sweet pepper and tomato soup is blended at the end. For this I use a hand blender so that I can put it straight into the saucepan, removing the need to wash a blender jug, something we all hate doing. I've added croutons and basil oil because, to me, they add a whole other dimension to the dish. You can, however, do without them and just make the soup to have with your favourite crusty bread. The soup itself is gluten-free, so all you need to do is change the bread to satisfy your dietary requirements.

Method

First heat the olive oil in a large saucepan and fry the onions and peppers together for 4-5 minutes, until they become slightly soft and the onions translucent. Add the garlic and fry for another minute, stirring continuously. Add the tomato puree, canned tomatoes, water and veg stock and bring to the boil. Turn down the heat and simmer for 20 minutes.

While this is cooking make your croutons. Preheat the oven to gas 6/200C/400F. Cut your ciabatta bread into 1 ½ cm cubes and place in a mixing bowl. Add the salt and oregano and toss the bread pieces to cover them. Then add the olive oil and mix in well with your hands to fully cover with the oil and seasoning. Place on a baking tray and cook on the top shelf of the oven for 15 minutes, or until brown and crisp. Set aside to cool.

Now make your basil oil by adding all the ingredients to a small blender and whizzing for a few seconds until you have a thick, green oil. You will need to stir it again before drizzling it on the soup.

Once the soup is cooked, use a hand blender to blend in the pan to a smooth consistency. If you are using a jug blender you will need to let the soup cool first. Once this is done, stir in the cream and bring back up to serving temperature and adjust seasoning as required. Do not continue to boil the soup with the cream in as it will separate. Serve the soup into bowls and top with the croutons, then drizzle the basil oil around the edge.

SHREDDED KALE WITH CHERRY TO-MATOES AND TAMARI DRESSING

Prep time: 5 minutes.
Cooking time: 10 minutes.

Serves 2

Ingredients:

250g black kale, cut into thin strips
3 cloves garlic, peeled and cut into thick slices of about 2mm
10 cherry tomatoes, halved
2 tbsp sesame oil.
For the Dressing:
3 tbsp tamari (gluten free soy sauce)
2 tbsp sweet chilli sauce
1 tbsp lime juice.

This side dish is super quick to make and will go with just about any Asian main you care to make.

Method:

Heat the sesame oil in a non-stick pan and fry the kale for 5 minutes or until slightly wilted. Add the cherry tomatoes and garlic at the same time and fry on a medium heat for a further 5 minutes, stirring occasionally. To make the dressing mix together the tamari, sweet chilli sauce and lime juice. Put the kale mixture into a bowl to serve and pour over the dressing. Serve warm.

PLANTAIN WITH CHICKPEAS

GLUTEN-FREE

Prep time: 10 minutes.
Cooking time: 10-12 minutes.

Serves 2.

Ingredients:

50g gram flour, for dusting
1 ripe plantain, sliced
4 tbsp groundnut oil
1 can chickpeas, washed, drained and placed on a towel to dry
2 cloves garlic, chopped
Salt and pepper to taste
Handful parsley leaves, chopped
Juice of ½ lemon

Put the gram flour in a container with a lid. Add the sliced plantain and gently shake until all the slices are coated in the flour. Heat 3 tbsp of the oil in a pan and fry the dusted plantain for about 3 minutes on each side, until browned. Sprinkle with some sea salt, then remove from the pan and set aside.

Heat the remaining tablespoon of oil in the pan and fry the chickpeas for about 3 minutes, stirring often. Add the garlic and fry for one more minute, then season with salt and pepper and put in the chopped parsley. Cook for a minute more, put the plantain back in and squeeze the lemon juice over the top. Toss the food in the pan to coat with the lemon juice, then serve.

SWEET POTATO ROSTIS

Prep Time: 10 minutes.
Cooking time: 6 minutes per batch, plus 10 minutes in the oven.

Serves 4

Ingredients:

3 medium sweet potatoes, peeled and grated
1 medium red onion, thinly sliced
40g walnuts, chopped
1 tsp garlic puree
½ tsp harissa paste (make sure it's gluten-free)
3 tbsp sweet barbecue sauce
½ tsp salt
Juice of half and orange
3 tbsp gram flour
Oil for frying.

The rosti is a good way of doing something a little different with your potatoes. They require forming a mixture with grated potato, binding it together and cooking as a patty. There are endless possibilities when it comes to your mix and, in this recipe, I've gone for a mildly sweet barbeque flavour. The sweet potato is quite dry when compared to the regular potato, which you would have to squeeze out after grating. There is no need to do this here. In fact, you will have to add more moisture in order to bind it together, which I've done with orange juice and barbeque sauce. Fry them in hot oil, and press down during cooking with a spatula from time to time to help them hold their shape.

Method

Heat the oven to gas 6/200C/400F.

Put all the ingredients, apart from the oil, into a mixing bowl and mix together with a large spoon. Heat a tablespoon of oil in a frying pan and put about 2 tablespoons of the rosti mixture into the palm of your hand. Press together with your other hand and make into a small flat round. Place it in the pan and repeat this another three or four times, remembering not to overcrowd the pan.

Cook the batch for three minutes on the one side, pressing down with the spatula occasionally to get them into shape, then gently turn them over to do the other side. Give them another three minutes, or until both side are golden brown, then place the batch on a baking tray.

Repeat the process until the tray is full of the rostis. Place the tray in the middle of the oven and cook for 10 minutes to finish them off.

SPICED PUMPKIN SEED HUMOUS

Prep time: 10 minutes.

Makes 750ml

Ingredients:

2 cans drained chickpeas
3 cloves garlic
3 tsp Cajun spice
1 tsp cinnamon
Juice of 1 lemon
1 tsp ground paprika
¼ tsp ground cumin
100 ml olive oil
½ tsp salt
20g pumpkin seeds.

This is a slight alternative to the classic humous recipe. Orangey-red in colour, with crunchy pumpkin seeds in every bite and a background of Cajun spice.

Serve this on some rustic bread and you've got a delicious light snack. It'll keep for about 4 days.

Method:

Place all of the ingredients, except for the pumpkin seeds, into a blender and puree until completely smooth. Pour into a container, stir in the pumpkin seeds and store in the refrigerator until ready to eat.

BRAISED TOFU THAI CAKES

Prep time: 15 minutes.
Cooking time: 15 minutes.

Makes about 12 cakes.

Ingredients:

2 medium potatoes
1 can braised tofu, drained and shredded
2 spring onions, finely sliced
1 mild green chilli, deseeded and chopped
Small handful fresh parsley, chopped
½ tsp ground paprika
1 tsp hot madras curry powder
Juice of half a lime
½ tsp salt
2 tbsp dairy-free yoghurt
4 tbsp gram flour
Cracked black pepper to taste
Olive oil for frying.

This dish uses the same technique as the potato rosti and is a great way of doing something a little different with your spuds. It involves grating the raw potato and squeezing as much of the moisture out as you can so that you don't end up with a mushy, water-logged mixture that isn't going to fry. There are many variations you can make of these. I've used a Thai chilli theme but once you've got your basic potato and tofu mixture together you can pick what you like for the rest. Go nuts!

Method

First peel and grate the potatoes. Once that is done place them onto a clean tea towel, wrap them up and squeeze over the sink until you get as much water out as you can. The dryer the better. Empty the drained potatoes into a mixing bowl. Add all of the other ingredients except for the oil into the bowl and mix well.

Pre heat the oven to gas 6/220C/400F.

Heat a non-stick frying pan with about 2 tablespoons of olive oil and, using a desert spoon, place four balls of the mixture into the pan. These cakes are quite small, so don't add too much. Fry for a few minutes on one side and then turn them over. Do this a couple of time until golden brown on each side and then place on a baking tray. Fry in batches of four until the mixture has gone and then place them in the oven for 10 minutes to make sure the potato has cooked through.

SWEET POTATO BURGER

EASY TO MAKE GLUTEN-FREE

Makes 6-8 burger patties

Ingredients:

50g dried gluten-free vegan mince
Enough water to soak the mince
2 tbsp flaxseeds
8 tbsp water
2 sweet potatoes, peeled and grated
1 medium red onion, finely diced
2 tbsp ground paprika
1 tsp salt
1 tsp mild chilli powder
2 slices brown bread (or gluten-free equivalent) blended into breadcrumbs
2 tbsp buckwheat flour
1 tbsp wholegrain mustard
1 tbsp garlic puree
2 tbsp tamari (gluten-free soy sauce)
Coconut oil for shallow frying.

There's no end of choice when it comes to making your own burgers. In this recipe I've chosen sweet potato as the main ingredient. It grates perfectly and remains dry, so there's no need to squeeze it out afterwards. The mince I've used is a dried vegan and gluten-free mince which we use all the time at home. This recipe is not gluten-free, but can easily be made so by swapping the sliced bread for your favourite gluten-free variety.

Method

First soak the mince in the water for 10-15 minutes, until rehydrated, then drain thoroughly and set aside. At the same time mix the flaxseeds with the 8 tbsp water in a small bowl and leave for 10 minutes to form a gloopy mixture. When these are ready put all the ingredients, apart from the coconut oil, into a large mixing bowl and combine with a spoon. Leave to absorb moisture for 30 minutes and then shape into patties using either a ring mould or just your hands. Place the patties onto baking paper. Heat a teaspoon of the coconut oil in a frying pan and fry the patties, two at a time for about 8 minutes on a medium low heat. You will want to turn the patties every 2 minutes to stop them from burning and to make sure the burger is cooked through. Serve with your favourite burger buns and dressings.

Kale and Spinach Tabbouleh Sandwich

EASY TO MAKE
GLUTEN-FREE

Preparation time: 10 minutes. Chilling time: 1 hour.

Ingredients:

65g fresh baby spinach
50g chopped kale
100g cooked quinoa
2 cloves garlic
8 cherry tomatoes, quartered (orange rapture are also good)
1 medium carrot, grated
½ cucumber, diced
Handful of coriander, chopped
4 tbsp almond yoghurt
2 tbsp olive oil
Salt and black pepper
4 Pumpkin seed bread rolls (or rolls of your choosing)
8 baby gem lettuce leaves to serve

This is a beautifully light and flavoursome summer sandwhich, that's just bursting with goodness. You don't have to wait until the summer, though. Get stuck in whatever time of year it is. Just switch the bread to make it gluten-free.

Method:

Simply put all the ingredients, apart from the lettuce and the bread, into a large mixing bowl and combine. Cover and leave in the fridge for one hour for the flavours to amalgamate. Cut the bread and put a small drizzle of olive oil on each side. Place two gem lettuce leaves on the bottom layer, then put a large spoonful of the tabbouleh onto the lettuce, put on the top layer of bread and enjoy.

GREEN PEA PASTA SALAD WITH PAN-FRIED PEACHES

GLUTEN-FREE

Prep time: 20 minutes.
Cooking time: 25 minutes.
Cooling time: 1-2 hours.

Serves 2 as a main, 4 as a side dish.

Ingredients:

For the Peaches:
3 Saturn peaches (regular peaches are also fine)
1 tbsp olive oil
2 tbsp brown sugar
Juice of half a lemon

For the Pasta Salad:
250g dried green pea pasta
One red Romano pepper, halved, deseeded and finely sliced
1 red onion, halved and finely sliced
1 x 3 inch length of cucumber, diced
1 tbsp flaked almonds
Salt to taste

For the Dressing:
3 tbsp olive oil
1 tbsp cider vinegar
1 tsp wholegrain mustard.

This is a cold dish, but with the peaches being pan-fried you have the option of serving them either hot or cold. For this recipe I have chosen to chill them. Another good thing about this is that it can be made the night before and taken to work the next day to have for lunch.

Method

Bring a pan of water to the boil and pour in the dried pasta. Boil for 8-10 minutes, depending on how firm you like it. 8 minutes is quite al dente, but 10 minutes still keeps it reasonably firm. Once the pasta is done (you can check by taking one out with a spoon and eating it) drain and plunge straight into cold water to completely cool.

Next you want to prepare the peaches. Cut each peach into quarters around the stone and prize apart, exactly as you would an avocado. Heat a frying pan with the tablespoon of oil and cook the peaches for 10 minutes, stirring occasionally, until soft and golden. Add the brown sugar and lemon juice and cook for a further 4-5 minutes. The peaches will become glazed as the sauce evaporates. Set aside to cool.

To make the salad, drain the now cold pasta completely, place into a mixing bowl and add all the other salad ingredients.

In a small dish, blend the olive oil, cider vinegar and wholegrain mustard with a whisk to make an emulsified dressing, then pour over the salad. Add the peaches once they have cooled and mix the salad together. Chill in the fridge for an hour or two before serving.

BRAISED CABBAGE WITH BLACK-EYED BEANS AND TOASTED PUMPKIN SEEDS

Prep time: 5 minutes (longer if you're using dried beans). Cooking time: 25 minutes.

Serves 4

Ingredients:

2 tbsp olive oil
190g pack ready cut fresh cabbage, washed and drained
250g black-eyed beans (canned or dried). If using dried, soak and cook them according to the recipe at the begining of this book. Canned beans should be drained.
1 tsp garlic puree
1 tsp wholegrain mustard
200ml veg stock
A small handful of pumpkin seeds
Salt and pepper to taste.

This is a delicately flavoured side dish that makes good use of fresh cabbage and either dried or canned beans. It's also meant to be made with little effort, which is why I've chosen to use ready-cut cabbage and garlic puree. This dish is ideal for after work, when you don't want much fuss in the kitchen. If the pan you're using doesn't have a lid for braising, then do what I did: put foil over the top of the pan and hold it in place with a chopping board.

You can sprinkle the pumpkin seeds straight from the packet if you like, but they are better if you toast them first by frying them in a dry pan for a minute or two on a medium heat. The seeds are ready when they begin to crackle, but be careful not to let them burn.

Method

Heat the oil in a pan and put the cabbage and beans in together. Fry for 5-6 minutes, until the cabbage has wilted and any water has evaporated. Add the garlic and mustard and fry for another two minutes. Pour in the veg stock and cover the pan with a lid. Simmer for 10-15 minutes, until the cabbage is cooked and most of the liquid has gone.

Turn off the heat but leave the lid on, then heat a small frying pan without any oil. Toast the pumpkin seeds for about 2 minutes, moving them often. They are ready when they begin to crackle but before they brown. Season the cabbage to taste, serve, and sprinkle the pumpkin seeds on top.

Scrumptious Focaccia Bread

Breadmaking is a very satisfying thing to be able to do, and it's something I've always been into. Focaccia bread is, in my opinion, one of the easiest breads to make, as you place it down on the baking tray without much in the way of shaping it. You still need to get your technique right, if you want the bread to rise properly and be light and airy. Dried yeast is available in every baking department in every supermarket. A lot of recipes tell you to mix the yeast straight in with the flour, but I always take the extra step of activating it beforehand. To do this you just mix the yeast with a small amount of tepid water and ½ a teaspoon of sugar, and let it rest for 15 minutes (I usually do this in a coffee mug). This technique not only gives you a better response from the yeast but also lets you know that it is still working. After resting for the allotted time, the yeast will become light and foamy and have increased in size. If this does not happen then it is no good and should not be used.

Kneading is something that takes a little practice. All dough-kneading is sticky and messy at the beginning but, if you've got your proportions correct, it will smooth out as you go along. It generally takes 10-15 minutes to properly knead bread so that it is stretchy and elastic in texture, which can seem like quite a long time when you're doing it. Persevere, because the more thorough your kneading, the better your bread will be. There are two stages of proving to be done, both in a warm place in your house, such as an airing cupboard or near a radiator. The first one takes about an hour and a half, where the dough will double in size. After this is the knocking back process, in which you hit the dough with your fists to knock all the air back out of it. Once you have done this it is time to shape your bread on or in the container you intend to cook it, and add any extra ingredients (in this case rosemary, sea salt and olive oil). Now you prove it again, this time only for about 20 minutes, in which time it will become pretty much the size of the finished loaf.

This is not an essential step, but I always spray the inside of the oven with water from a spray bottle before putting bread in. It adds a little humidity and helps to avoid burning the crust.

If you've not made bread before, this one is a good place to start, as it is about as easy as homemade bread gets. I hope you have fun with it.

Prep time: 30 minutes. Proving time: Up to 2 hours. Cooking time: 25 minutes, plus cooling time.

Makes 1 large or 2 small loaves.

Ingredients:

2 tsp (10-12g) lose, or 2 sachets of dried yeast
½ tsp sugar
450 ml lukewarm water, a small amount is for the yeast mixture
650g strong white bread flour, plus more for kneading
2 tsp sea salt, plus extra before cooking
3 tbsp olive oil, plus extra for greasing and brushing
1 sprig fresh rosemary, chopped.

You will also need a water spray gun to add moisture to the oven, if you are using this method.

Put the yeast in a mug or small bowl, add the sugar and then enough water to cover the yeast. Mix this with a spoon and set aside for 15 minutes. It will turn foamy after a while.

Put the flour and salt into a large mixing bowl and combine. Add the yeast when it is ready, and the olive oil. Bring all the ingredients together, either with your hands or a table knife, until a dough starts to form. Mix for a minute or so with your hands to really bring it together. Now add a little flour to your work surface and put the dough onto it. It will still be quite sticky at this time. Knead with both hands, stretching, folding and turning the dough repeatedly, adding a little more flour when it sticks too much to the surface. Keep this going for about 10-15 minutes, until you have a smooth elastic dough that doesn't stick so much to the hands.

Put a little olive oil in a clean mixing bowl and turn the dough around in it to coat it in the oil. Cover the bowl with a clean tea towel and leave in a warm place for about 1 ½ hours, until it has doubled in size.

Grease a large baking tray with olive oil.

Bring the dough back to your floured surface and press and punch all the air out of it. This is the knocking back process, where you are bringing the dough back to the state it was in before it was proven. Place the dough on the baking tray and form a large oval with your hands. Press all of your fingers into the top of the dough to create the indents that you see in focaccia bread, then brush with more olive oil and sprinkle with sea salt and the chopped rosemary. Cover the dough again with the towel and put it back in the warm place for another 20 minutes, until it is about 1 ½ times its size.

Preheat the oven to gas 7/220C/425F.

When the dough is ready, open the oven door and spray water a couple of time into it to create a slightly moist atmosphere. Two sprays will do it. Gently put the bread into the middle of the oven and cook for 25 minutes, until it is risen and browned. Allow to cool on the baking tray for about 10 minutes and then transfer to a cooling rack. Before serving, brush with more olive oil and sea salt if required.

Broccoli, Courgette and 'Blue Cheese' Soup

GLUTEN-FREE

Prep time: 10 minutes.
Cooking time: 25 minutes.

Serves 4-6

Ingredients:

1.5 litres veg stock (make
sure it's gluten-free)
1 large broccoli head,
including stalk, cut into
small pieces
1 courgette, diced
2 cloves garlic, smashed
120g vegan blue-style
cheese (I used the Tesco
Free From one), chopped
or grated

Bring the stock to the boil in a large saucepan. Add all the ingredients apart from the cheese and simmer, with a lid on, for 10 minutes, until the vegetables are tender. Take off the heat and use either a hand or jug blender to puree the soup. I find the hand blenders easier for soups, as you can puree them in the saucepan and you don't have to let it cool first. Once it is fully smooth, put the soup back on the heat and add the cheese. Simmer for 10 more minutes and then blend again. Serve with your favourite crusty bread.

Pan-Fried Plum and Avocado Salad

Prep time: 10 minutes.
Cooking time: 5 minutes.

Serves 2.

Ingredients:

120g mixed salad leaves
½ red onion, thinly sliced
8 baby plum or cherry tomatoes, halved
½ cucumber, diced
1 ripe avocado, diced
1 tbsp lemon juice
Pinch sea salt
4 ripe plums, halved and stoned
1 tbsp rapeseed oil
1 tbsp soft brown sugar

Warm fruit on a cold salad is a winning combination. It adds contrast and depth, and it instantly raises it above a standard salad. For this recipe I've used pan-fried plums, which are caramelised in a little brown sugar. That's the only cooking involved in this dish. The rest is just raw ingredients thrown together. You can use any salad leaves you like for this, either pre-prepped, or you can chop up your own with whatever you've got hanging around.

Method:

In a large mixing bowl, put the salad leaves, red onion, tomatoes and cucumber. Mix the diced avocado with the lemon juice and put that in the salad bowl also, then season with a pinch of sea salt and mix the salad together. You can use any of the dressings from this book at this point to mix in with the salad. I used the grape and balsamic vinegar dressing (page:)

Heat the oil in a frying pan and fry the plums for about 3 minutes, turning with cooking tongs, until starting to soften and brown. Turn them cut side up and sprinkle the brown sugar over them, then flip them back over and cook them for another minute or so, until they have caramelised. Divide the salad onto two plates and place 4 plum halves on top of each salad.

MUSHROOM, SPINACH AND TOFU BURGER

GLUTEN-FREE

Prep time: 15-20 minutes.
Cooking time: 25 minutes.

Makes 8 patties.

Ingredients:

1 small red onion,
chopped
100g mushrooms, chopped
4 tbsp groundnut, or similar, oil, plus more if needed
1 X 400g block tofu,
drained
200g red kidney beans,
cooked (or from a can)
100g cooked brown rice
1 tsp yeast extract
1 tsp wholegrain mustard
¼ tsp harissa paste
3 tbsp tamari (gluten-free
soy sauce)
400g frozen spinach
(weight when frozen)
thawed and drained
70g soya flour (or other
gluten-free flour)

Heat the oil in a pan and saute the onions and mushrooms for about 3 minutes, until mostly cooked.
Remove from the pan and set aside. Put all the other
ingredients up to, and including, the tamari into a
food-processor and blend to a mostly smooth but still
a little chunky mixture. Empty into a mixing bowl
and add the squeezed-out spinach. Add the onions,
mushrooms and flour and mix well. Shape the mixture into burger shapes (should make 8).

Preheat the oven to gas 6/200C/400F

Heat another tablespoon of oil in the pan and fry 2
of the patties for 4 minutes each side, until golden
brown. Add a little more oil if necessary. Repeat until
all the patties are gone and then cook them on a tray
in the oven for 10 minutes to finish off.

CLASSIC TOMATO SOUP

GLUTEN-FREE

Prep time: 5 minutes.
Cooking time: about 30 minutes.

Serves 4

Ingredients:

2 tbsp olive oil
1 medium onion, diced
1 tsp garlic puree
3 large plum tomatoes, roughly chopped
2 veg stock cubes (gluten-free)
2 cans chopped tomatoes
2 cans water
2 tbsp vegan Worcester sauce
2 tbsp soft brown sugar
Salt and pepper to taste

This is quick and easy comfort food for any time of day. This recipe will give you a delicious homemade tomato soup that tastes better than anything out of a can, and it'll give it to you in about 30 minutes. True, it's not as quick as opening a can and heating it up, but the difference is vast.

Even before I became vegan I hadn't opened a can of soup in years. The simple reason is that it's not only easy to make soup, it's easy to make great soup. Once you realise this, it might be a cold day in hell before you open a can of the stuff also.

Method:

Heat the oil in a saucepan and fry the onions for 5 minutes, until soft and translucent. Add the garlic and cook for a minute longer, then put in the fresh chopped tomatoes and cook for 4 more minutes, stirring often.

Add the veg stock cubes, stir in and put in the canned tomatoes. Fill the empty cans back up with water and pour that in as well. Add the Worcester sauce and sugar and bring to the boil.

Turn down the heat and simmer for about 20-25 minutes, then blend until smooth. If you are using a jug blender and the soup is still hot, then make sure steam can escape.

Season to taste and serve with your favourite bread.

GARLIC MUSHROOMS WITH POLENTA

GLUTEN-FREE

Prep time: 20 minutes.
Cooking time: 35-45 minutes. Cooling time: 1-2 hours.

Serves 4

Ingredients:

For the Polenta:
1.5 litres light vegetable stock (gluten-free)
250g course corn meal (polenta)
Olive oil for greasing

For the Garlic Mushrooms:
500g chestnut mushrooms, quartered
3 tbsp olive oil
4 cloves garlic, chopped
2 tsp corn flour (gluten-free)
1 tsp wholegrain mustard
250ml dairy-free milk
Salt and pepper to taste
You will also need extra olive oil for frying the polenta.

Polenta is one of my favourite staples, particularly when it is cut into triangles and fried in a little olive oil, as it is with this recipe. It gives it a crisp outer coating, but remains gooey in the middle. The polenta can be made in advance and cooled, ready for frying before serving it.

Making fresh polenta can be quite hard work, as there is a lot of whisking, but it really is worth the effort. The trick is to bring the water to the boil and then whisk the polenta flour in in a steady stream. Keep the water spinning as you're pouring and you will have very few lumps in your final dish. Polenta thickens very quickly, so you will need to whisk it quite often to prevent it from sticking to the pan. It also spits, so I turn it down to a low simmer for 15 minutes to cook it through. It will still spit, so watch your hands.

This is served with a very basic garlic mushrooms poured over the top. It's a delicious mid-week meal that isn't heavy on the stomach, leaving you room for dessert!

Method

Grease an oven dish with olive oil and set aside.

In a large saucepan, bring the vegetable stock to the boil and whisk to form a whirlpool. Steadily pour in the polenta while continuing to whisk to get the lumps out. The polenta will start to thicken straight away. Bring back to the boil and simmer for 15 minutes, whisking frequently. Once the polenta is cooked, pour it into the oven dish and smooth it out with a spatula. Set aside and leave to cool and set for an hour or two.

Once it is set, cut the polenta first into squares, and then triangles.
Preheat the oven to Gas 3/170C/325F.

Heat a tablespoon or so of olive oil in a non-stick pan and fry 4 polenta triangles at a time, for about 4-5 minutes each side, until they are slightly browned and crispy. Do as many batches as you need and keep them warm in the oven.

Now make the garlic mushrooms. Heat the oil in a non-stick pan or wok and sautee the mushrooms on a high heat, until they are browned. Add the garlic and cook for 2 more minutes, then mix in the corn flour and mustard. Gradually pour in the milk, stirring as you go. Season to taste and simmer for about 4-5 minutes, until you have a thick sauce.

To serve, place 2-3 polenta triangles on a plate and then spoon some of the garlic mushrooms on top.

Salad of Spinach, Brown, Rice, Hazelnuts and Avocado

Prep time: 15 minutes, plus soaking and chilling the rice. Cooking time: 20 minutes for the rice.

Serves 2 as a main.

Ingredients:

80g baby spinach, washed
400g cooked brown basmati rice, chilled
65g dried mixed berries
60g whole hazelnuts
1 ripe avocado, diced
3 tbsp tamari (gluten free)
2 tbsp sesame oil
Juice of ½ lemon.

This is a bit of a power salad, created to give an extra fibre boost, as well as being totally delicious. Cook the rice an hour or so beforehand, to make sure it's fully chilled by the time the salad is finished. Just refer to my recipe on cooking brown basmati rice. It's gluten-free, so anybody can enjoy it. You can also omit the sesame oil if you want to keep it oil free, but I find it adds a delicate nutty flavour to the rice. You can also switch it for groundnut oil if you want something flavourless.

The recipe is for two as a main course, but it will also serve four as a starter or side. The dried berries you can get from most supermarkets. I chose a small mixed tub, but you can trade them for whatever you can find. Cranberries or blueberries would go very well.

Method

All you do with this is put everything into a large mixing bowl and stir with a spoon until fully combined. Serve immediately.

Veggie Tofu Omelette

Prep time: 15 minutes.
Cooking time: about 35 minutes, plus 10 minutes resting time.

Serves 4

Ingredients:

For the veggies:
2 tbsp olive oil
180g block of plain tofu
150g mushrooms, sliced
½ leek, sliced
1 large or 2 small tomatoes, cut into wedges
100g shredded kale, washed and stalks removed
200g washed spinach leaves
2 tbsp nutritional yeast
Salt and pepper to taste

For the omelette batter:
5 heaped tbsp gram flour
300ml almond milk
2 tsp English mustard
Salt and pepper to taste
1 tbsp olive oil for frying

If you think that turning vegan will deny you the pleasures of a good omelette, then think again. This one is a twist on the classic Spanish omelette, made with gram flour and tofu, and packed full of vegetables for a great taste and high nutritional value. It's made by stir frying the vegetables first and then pouring them into the omelette batter, before cooking the whole thing in a pan. It is best cooked on a lower heat, as it needs to become solid most of the way through before you turn it. This can take at least 10 minutes to achieve, so a lower heat will prevent the bottom burning during that time.

The best way to flip this omelette over is to use a plate. Trying to turn this with your spatula is only going to end in tears. To do this you put a plate over the top of the omelette, hold it firmly in place, and then flip the pan over. If all has gone well when you remove the pan you will have the cooked side facing up and the raw side face down on the plate. From here you simply slide the omelette back into the pan. It does take a bit of courage if you haven't done it before but, as long as the dish is cooked most of the way through and the plate is held firmly in place, you won't go far wrong.

Method:

First squeeze all the moisture out of the tofu by wrapping it in a clean towel and putting a heavy saucepan on it. Leave for 10 minutes.

While the tofu is draining, you can make the omelette batter. Put the flour into a mixing bowl and add the milk a little at a time, whisking as you go to beat the lumps out. When all the milk is in and you have a smooth batter, whisk in the mustard and generously season. Set aside.

Once the tofu is drained, cut it into small cubes. Heat the 2 tablespoons of olive oil in a large pan or wok and fry the mushrooms for about 4 minutes. Add the tofu and leeks and fry for another five minutes. Use a wooden spoon or spatula to break up the tofu further as it is cooking. When it is starting to brown add the tomato wedges and cook for another 2 minutes. Put the kale and spinach in the pan and cover with a lid (tin foil with a chopping board placed on top work well if your pan doesn't have one). Turn down the heat and cook for 5 minutes, or until the greens have wilted, then take the lid off and turn the heat back up. Add the nutritional yeast and season with salt and pepper. Cook on a high heat until almost all the liquid from steaming has evaporated.

When the veggies are ready, let them cool for 5 minutes and then tip them into the omelette batter. Mix to fully incorporate.

Heat the tablespoon of olive oil in a frying pan, until quite hot, and then pour the omelette mixture in. Turn down the heat and cook for about 10 minutes, until it has set most of the way through. You can move the omelette a little during this time. Use your spatula to tuck in the sides and loosen the bottom while it is cooking. This will make it easier when it comes to turning it over. When it is solid about three-quarters of the way through, take a plate large enough to completely cover the omelette and place it firmly down on top of it. You should be holding the pan in one hand and be securing the bottom of the plate with the other. In one quick, smooth motion, flip the pan over with the plate still holding the omelette tightly in place. Put the plate down on your worktop and gently lift off the frying pan. You should now have the cooked side of the omelette facing upwards.

Clean any excess off the pan and put it back on the heat, adding a little more oil. Slide the omelette off the plate, back into the pan. Cook this for another 5 minutes or so, until fully set and browned on the bottom. Turn off the heat and allow it to sit in the pan for 5-10 minutes to rest, then cut into quarters and serve.

Sweet Potato and Asparagus Wraps

Prep time: 10 minutes. Cooking time: 45 minutes.

Makes 4.

Ingredients:

For the roasted sweet potatoes:
3 small sweet potatoes, peeled and cut into large chunks
2 tbsp olive oil
2 tbsp smoky sweet BBQ sauce
Pinch sea salt

For the dressing:
75g vegan mayonnaise
1 tbsp lemon juice
1 tbsp vegan pesto

For the Filling:
2 tbsp olive oil
6 sweet mini peppers, deseeded and halved (or 2 regular peppers, cut into 8 pieces each)
200g asparagus, hard, woody part of the stem cut off
Pinch sea salt
8 baby plum or cherry tomatoes, halved

4 wholemeal or gluten-free wraps

Preheat the oven to gas 7/220C/425F.

Put the sweet potatoes in a bowl and pour over the olive oil and BBQ sauce. Sprinkle on the sea salt and mix thoroughly. Pour the potatoes out onto a baking tray and cook at the top of the oven for about 35 minutes, or until browned and soft. Give them a mix up halfway through the cooking.

Meanwhile, make the dressing by putting all the dressing ingredients into a small bowl and stirring with a fork to combine.

10 minutes before the potatoes have finished cooking, heat the 2 tablespoons of olive oil in a frying pan or wok and cook the asparagus and peppers together for 8-10 minutes, or until browned and al dente. Season with the sea salt during cooking.

Once the potatoes and veg are cooked you can start assembling the wraps. To do this, lay one wrap out on a plate and line a quarter of the potatoes across the middle, leaving about an inch free at one end for folding. Next put on a quarter of the asparagus, peppers and raw tomatoes and spoon on some of the dressing. Fold the back end that you left free and then gently roll the wrap over the vegetables. Do this with the other three wraps and serve.

SIDES & SNACKS

BABY NEW POTATOES WITH GARLIC AND CHILLI

GLUTEN FREE

Prep time: 5 minutes.
Cooking time: 30 minutes

Serves 4 – 6

Ingredients:

1kg baby new potatoes
1 red chilli, deseeded and sliced
3 cloves of garlic, peeled and thickly sliced (about 2mm)
Half a handful of fresh parsley
2 tbsp olive oil
Salt and black pepper.

These are very simple baby new potatoes, boiled until tender and then pan-fried. A non-stick wok is the best tool for this if you have one as there's plenty of room for the potatoes to move around as they are cooking.

Method:

Put the new potatoes into a pan of cold water and bring to the boil. Simmer for about 15 minutes until the potatoes are tender when pierced with a sharp knife. Drain them off and allow to cool slightly.

Heat the olive oil in a large frying pan or wok then add the potatoes. Pan fry for 10 minutes until the potato skins are golden in colour. Add the garlic and chilli and fry for 4 more minutes. When the garlic is just starting to brown add the parsley and fry for another minute or two, season with the salt and pepper and serve straight away.

Very Berry Protein Bars

Prep time: 15 minutes.
Cooking time 5 minutes.
Chilling time 2-3 hours.

Makes about 20 bars.

Ingredients:

200g pitted dates, roughly chopped, either by hand or in a food processor
50g flaked almonds
70g almond butter
30g pumpkin seeds
150g oats
40g (1 scoop) pea protein
20g ground flaxseeds
75ml maple syrup
200g frozen or fresh berries (I used forest fruit)
40g vegan margarine, plus extra for greasing

These are great little protein and fibre bars for when you're on the go. Just pack a couple in your lunchbox and you've got an extra boost to keep you going between meals. The sugar in these comes entirely from maple syrup and dates and is kept to a minimum to allow the other flavours to come out. I've used frozen forest fruit berries for this, but you can use any of the packs of frozen fruit available in the supermarkets. You can also use fresh if you prefer. Because of the berries, it is better to keep the bars chilled when storing them and just take what you want as you need them.
I buy my pea protein from myprotein.com, but they are becoming more and more widely available now and I have seen smaller packets in supermarkets.

Method:

Grease a small baking tray with a little margarine and line it with greaseproof paper, making sure you take the paper up over the edges.

Put all the ingredients, apart from the berries and the margarine into a large mixing bowl and mix together until fully incorporated. In a small saucepan, heat the berries and margarine together and simmer for 5 minutes, until the berries have softened, and you have a sauce. Pour this into the mixing bowl with the rest of the ingredients and mix thoroughly.

Spoon the mixture into the baking tray and press down with the back of the spoon until it is flat and tight into the corners. Cover and put in the fridge for 2-3 hours to set.

Once it is set, turn the tray upside down onto a chopping board, so that the block falls out. Carefully remove the paper and cut the block down the middle lengthways. Make 8 or 9 widthways cuts, to produce 18-20 bars, then store back in the fridge. They'll last about a 5 days.

QUICK AND EASY GUACAMOLE

GLUTEN-FREE

Prep time: 10 minutes.
Chilling time: 2 hours.

Serves 4

Ingredients:

8 ripe Has avocados, cut
in half lengthways and the
stones removed
3 tbsp lemon juice
1 mild red chilli, deseeded
and finely chopped
½ small red onion, finely
diced
¼ tsp salt
A handful of chopped
coriander
¼ tsp garlic granules
¼ tsp ground cumin
A pinch of cayenne pepper
4 baby plum or cherry to-
matoes, finely diced.

For me, Guacamole is a humble dish that has some
depth but where the main ingredient – the avocado –
shines through. It should be clean and fresh, not over
salty or too spicy, with just a touch of lemon. I hope
you try this version which, for me, represents its
unique and subtle flavour. Make this dish two hours
ahead of time and serve the same day as it doesn't
keep very well.

Method:

Scoop out the avocado flesh from the skin with a desert spoon (this will be easy with ripe fruit) and place
them in a mixing bowl, or saucepan if you prefer a
flat surface. Immediately pour on the lemon juice and
toss the avocadoes to coat them. Take a potato masher and mash the avocadoes until they are thick and
mushy with a few small lumps remaining, then add
all the ingredients apart from the tomatoes and mix
well. When that is done add the tomatoes and gently
fold into the mixture to not disturb them too much.
Finally place in an air-tight container and chill in the
fridge for two hours before serving.

Curried Potatoes with White Kidney Beans and Chilli

Prep time: 10 minutes.
Cooking time: 15 minutes

Serves 4 as a side dish.

Ingredients:

3 tbsp rapeseed oil
2 large potatoes, diced
with the skin on, cooked
and drained
2 cans white kidney beans,
drained
1 red chilli, deseeded and
finely sliced
2 cloves garlic, sliced
1 tsp cumin seeds
½ tsp turmeric
1 tsp ground coriander
1 tsp tandoori masala curry powder
½ tsp salt
Small handful of coriander
leaves, chopped
Juice of half a lemon.

This is a spicy side dish that will go with any Indian main course. The recipe is dry, which will add a nice contrast to a meal that has more sauce. You can also have it on its own, perhaps with my masala sauce recipe. The potatoes should be cooked until tender before frying, or they will be too firm in the finished dish. You can do this either in a saucepan, or in a microwavable bowl with a lid and a small amount of water. Just remember that you want them tender, not overcooked. The white kidney beans you can get from the world food section of most supermarkets. Cannellini beans will do as a substitute if you can't get hold of them.

Method

Heat the oil in a frying pan or wok and sauté the cooked potatoes for 6-8 minutes, until starting to brown. Add the cumin seeds and cook for another minute, then add the beans and cook for 3 minutes more. Put in the garlic and chilli and fry for another minute. Stir often to make sure that nothing sticks. Drizzle on a little more oil if necessary, then put in the rest of the spices and the salt. Mix this all in and fry for a couple more minutes to intensify the flavours. Just before you stop cooking, add the chopped coriander and lemon juice and stir in.

Oven Roasted Apricots

Gluten-Free

Prep time: 10 minutes.
Cook time 30-40 minutes

Ingredients:

600g ripe apricots, stoned and halved
2 tbsp olive oil
2 tbsp ground cinnamon
½ tsp ground mixed spice
pinch cayenne pepper
2 tbsp unrefined sugar.

Have these as a desert or simply as a snack. Served hot or cold, these apricots are easy to cook and amazing to eat.

Method:

Preheat the oven to gas mark 6/200C/400F

Put all of your ingredients into a large mixing bowl and mix together with your hands until evenly combined. Place on a baking tray with the flesh side up and cook in the oven for 30 – 40 minutes, or until the edges have started to brown. Allow to cool for 5 minutes or so before serving, or cool completely and then chill for 2 hours.

MAPLE SPICED CASHEW NUTS

GLUTEN-FREE

Prep time: 2 minutes.
Cooking time: 4 minutes.
Cooling time: 4-5 minutes

Serves 2-3

Ingredients:

1 tsp ground paprika
¼ tsp mild chilli powder
½ tsp cinnamon
½ tsp ground cumin
¼ tsp salt
1 tbsp rapeseed oil
200g plain cashew nuts
2 tbsp maple syrup

This is a quick little snack that will hopefully stop you reaching for the salted peanuts every time you're peckish. They take about four minutes to cook and about the same to cool, so they are super-fast and just a little bit healthier than pre-made packet nuts. You have to watch them constantly though, as they burn easily.

Method:

Put all the dry spices into a bowl and keep to hand.

Heat the oil in a frying pan and fry the cashew nuts for about 3 minutes, shaking them often to prevent burning and encourage even cooking. Add the spices, mix thoroughly and cook for a minute more, then pour on the maple syrup. Stir the nuts in the pan to fully coat them, then turn them out onto a sheet of greaseproof paper to cool.

Leave them for 5 minutes before eating.

POTATO AND WILD ROCKET SALAD

GLUTEN-FREE

Prep time: 10 minutes.
Cooking time: 10-12 minutes.

Serves 4-6.

Ingredients:

4 large potatoes, peeled and cut into 8 pieces each
2 small red apples, cored and diced
75g sultanas
30g pumpkin seeds
50g wild rocket leaves
Salt and black pepper to taste
200g vegan blue cheese dressing (page 57)

I've been into potato salad since a very brief work stint at Pizza Hut over twenty years ago. I hated the job, in fact I only lasted three weeks, but I did like making the potato salad, which I did in a room downstairs, away from the busy Oxford Street chaos that was pizza service. There was nothing special about their salad, but I did get to eat a fair bit of it at the time, and for some reason I've had a soft spot for potato salad ever since.

I have come up with various potato salads over the years, and this is one of my favourites. It uses wild rocket leaves, as well as apple and sultanas for a sweeter flavour. The dressing is vegan blue cheese, which you can find on page… All in all it's a great side dish that you can enjoy all year round.

Method.

Fill a saucepan with cold water and put in the potatoes. Bring the water to the boil and then put a lid on and cook for 10-12 minutes, or until tender but not falling apart. Once they are cooked, strain and plunge the potatoes straight into cold water to stop them cooking any further and to cool them down.

Once the potatoes are cool, put them in a large mixing bowl with the rest of the ingredients and mix thoroughly. Keep the salad chilled until ready to serve.

BBQ Pineapple Steaks with Chilli and Plum Sauce

Prep time: 10 minutes. Marinade time: 30 minutes. Cooking time: 15-20 minutes.

Makes about 12 steaks.

Ingredients:

2 fresh pineapples, topped and tailed, peeled and cut into slices about 1½ cm thick

For the marinade:
3 tbsp plum sauce, fresh or bottled (page 56)
2 tbsp hoisin sauce
3 tbsp olive oil
2 tbsp cider vinegar
1 tsp mild chilli powder

Like a lot of men, I like to cook over open coals. Unfortunately, with the British weather the way it is, I don't get to do it all that often. When I do barbeque, I always make these pineapple steaks or some variation of them. My family love them and the plate is emptied every time they're put on the table. These are thick-cut slices of fresh pineapple, marinated in a sweet and hot sauce and cooked over hot coals. Don't worry if it's the wrong time of year, these will cook just as well on a griddle on the kitchen stove no matter what season it is.

Method:

Mix all the marinade ingredients together to form a thick sauce. Place the sliced pineapple into a large bowl and pour over the marinade. Mix around with your hands until the pineapple is completely coated and leave to marinade for at least 30 minutes. Place the slices on an already heated barbecue rack or a griddle and cook for 7-10 minutes on each side until soft and slightly browned. Serve immediately.

Cajun Spiced Popcorn

GLUTEN-FREE

Prep time: 2 minutes:
Cooking time: 10 minutes.

Serves 4

Ingredients:

2 tbsp sesame oil
½ cup dried popcorn kernels
1 tbsp vegan margarine
1 tbsp groundnut oil
1 tbsp Cajun seasoning
2 tbsp unrefined sugar
½ tsp cinnamon

You will also need a large saucepan with a lid.

The great thing about homemade popcorn is that it is one of the easiest dishes to make, and arguably the most fun. Not only that, but it is ridiculously cheap if you buy the kernels and cook them at home. The dried kernels are available in most supermarkets, usually with the dried beans or couscous, and they're quite often under a quid for 500g. With that, you can make buckets of it.

This recipe still gives you sweet popcorn, but with a spicy kick that keeps you coming back for more. Try them on your next movie night with friends. Better yet, make yourself a bucket-load and curl up on the sofa with it.

Method

Heat the sesame oil in the large saucepan under a medium heat and pour in the popcorn kernels. Put the lid straight on and shake the popcorn a little to stop it from burning. Do this every minute or so. It will take about 5 minutes before the kernels start popping, so don't worry if it feels like it's taking a long time. It will happen. Keep shaking every minute or so while the kernels are popping (you will need a tea-towel for this as the pan lid will be getting hot). The popcorn is ready when the popping is reduced to only one every 3 seconds or so. Remove from the heat and leave the lid on as some will continue to pop.

In a small saucepan heat the groundnut oil and butter until melted and add the sugar, Cajun spice and cinnamon. Simmer for about 20 seconds and then pour over the popcorn. Stir and shake until the popcorn is completely coated and serve immediately.

FRIED CABBAGE WITH 'BACON' AND EDAMAME BEANS

Prep time: 25 minutes. Cooking time: 25 minutes.

Serves 4

Ingredients:

2 tbsp olive oil, plus more if needed
4 rashers of vegan bacon, cut into small squares
2 cloves garlic, chopped
150g edamame beans
Handful pine nuts
600g sliced cabbage (pre-cooked weight), cooked, drained and cooled
2 tbsp white wine vinegar
3 tbsp tamari

This is a variation of the German fried cabbage and potatoes, using fake bacon and edamame beans. Pine nuts are also included to give it a nutty crunch, and it is flavoured with white wine vinegar and tamari. You can either prepare your own cabbage, or buy it ready-cut.

Method

Heat the oil in a large frying pan or wok. Add the bacon and cook for 5 minutes or so, until crisp but not burned. Add the garlic and cook for another minute, then add the beans and the pine nuts. Cook for 2 more minutes and then add the cabbage. Fry the whole mixture, adding more oil if needed, for 10 minutes, stirring occasionally, then pour in the vinegar and tamari. Cook for 2-3 more minutes to reduce any liquid and serve.

OVEN-ROASTED TOMATOES

GLUTEN-FREE

Prep time: 5 minutes. Cooking time: 34-45 minutes.

Makes 12

Ingredients:

6 large, ripe plum or salad tomatoes, cut in half
2 cloves garlic, chopped
1 tbsp fresh rosemary, chopped
3 tbsp olive oil
Pinch of sea salt and ground black pepper

These are a delicious and easy Mediterranean-style way of cooking tomatoes with minimum effort. They are a perfect side to have with your lunch and can be eaten hot or cold. They make a nice contrast when served warm with a salad, and they would go perfectly with my Roasted Fennel and Broccoli Quiche (page 162). I like to eat them by themselves, if I've made a batch and they're just lying around.

Method:

Preheat the oven to gas 6/200C/400F

Put all the ingredients into a mixing bowl and toss them around until the tomatoes are fully coated. Lay them cut side up on a baking tray and pour over any remaining oil and seasoning from the bowl. Place near the top of the oven and cook for 35-45 minutes, until the tomatoes have just started to char around the edges.

HOMEMADE ROAST POTATOES

GLUTEN-FREE

Prep time: 10 minutes.
Cooking time: just over an
hour. Cooling time: 15-20
minutes.

Serves 4-6

Ingredients:

2kg floury potatoes (Maris
Piper are good)
2 tbsp coconut oil
Pinch of flaky sea salt
Rosemary to garnish

Roast potatoes were something of a staple growing up in my house. We had them three or four days a week (no, I'm not exaggerating), because that was how much my father loved them. It was the same for him when he grew up, but I am happy to say that I have not carried on the family tradition. I love roast potatoes too, but I really don't want to live off them.

I don't make them as my father did. In my childhood he would use animal fat to roast them and now he uses vegetable oil. I prefer coconut oil for mine because it gives them a distinct and pleasant flavour, particularly at Christmas, when you want something a little special. Coconut oil is the vegan version of goose fat in this case. One technique I have stuck to all these years, however, is to parboil the potatoes first. For me, it is a step not to be missed. It ensures that the potato can be cooked at a high enough temperature to become crisp and still make sure it is cooked through. It also allows you to fluff them. Fluffing your potatoes is where you shake them in the colander prior to putting them in the oven. This gives them a rough and crumbly edge that will make really crispy potatoes.

Floury spuds are the key. Maris Piper, Desiree and King Edward are the ones used most often and every cook will have their favourite. Marfona are the only variety my father will use for his roasties. Maris piper are my chosen variety here, but I'm just as at home with the others. Feel free to experiment and find what suits you best.

Method

First have a large saucepan half filled with cold water on standby. Peel your potatoes and cut them in half, then put them straight into the water. Make sure there is enough water to cover the potatoes. Bring the pot to the boil and then continue to boil gently for about 6 minutes, until the potatoes are soft around the edges but not cooked all the way through. Drain the parboiled potatoes using a colander, reserving as much of the water as you can for gravy if you are making any. Leave the potatoes in the colander to cool for about 20 minutes.

While they are cooling preheat the oven to gas 6/200C/400F.

Fluff the cooled potatoes by shaking them gently in the colander, until they have a rough coating. Put the coconut oil onto a baking tray and heat in the oven until very hot. The potatoes should sizzle when you put them in the pan. Pour all of the potatoes into the pan, being careful not to splash yourself with the oil (I did exactly that during the making of these ones). Sprinkle with the sea salt and turn over to fully coat them. Cook near the top of the oven for 50 minutes to 1 hour, depending on how browned you like them. Turn them after 20 minutes or so, but not before, then turn them again, if necessary, 5 minutes or so before they are done. To serve, sprinkle with more sea salt and fresh rosemary.

BROCCOLI CHEESE

Prep time: 10 minutes.
Cooking time: about 45 minutes.

Serves 2-4.

Ingredients:

2 medium heads broccoli, cut into florets
1 batch vegan cheese sauce (page 51)
Vegan margarine for greasing
Salt and pepper to taste
100g vegan cheese, grated
1 tbsp coarse cornmeal (polenta)

This is a quick and easy alternative to cauliflower cheese that you can either have as a main course or a side dish. I often serve mine with a Sunday roast to add an extra dimension, but it goes well with a variety of dishes.

Method:

Bring a pan of water to the boil and cook the broccoli for 5 minutes, so that it is still slightly firm and vibrant green. Drain and run immediately under cold water to stop the cooking process.

Preheat the oven to gas 6/200C/400F and grease an oven dish with the margarine.

Put the broccoli in the dish and pour over the cheese sauce. Mix to fully coat, season with the salt and pepper, and then sprinkle the grated cheese over the top. Finally, sprinkle over the cornmeal and bake in the middle of the oven for 35-45 minutes, until browned.

Cinnamon and Chilli Spiced Oven Roasted Carrots

GLUTEN-FREE

Prep time: 5 minutes.
Cooking time: 40 minutes.

Serves 4

Ingredients:

800g fresh carrots, topped, tailed and peeled
1 tbsp sesame oil
1 tsp ground cinnamon
¼ tsp allspice
1 tsp paprika
1 tsp chilli oil (or ½ tsp chilli powder)
1 tbsp maple syrup
½ tsp balsamic vinegar
Pinch sea salt

If I'm going to have carrots as a side dish, then I usually like to have them roasted. This version gives them a real cinnamon taste but with a little bit of a kick (which, of course, is optional if chilli isn't your thing). The chilli oil used in this recipe is the jarred kind that you get in Chinese supermarkets, basically consisting of vegetable oil, salt and chilli flakes. It's hot stuff so go easy with it. If you can't get it just use ½ a teaspoon of chilli powder instead. Super quick to prep, this dish is a great accompaniment to any Sunday roast.

Method

Preheat the oven to Gas 7/220C/425F.

First cut the carrots into thick batons by cutting them in half widthways, then half lengthways and half lengthways again. Put the batons into a large mixing bowl and put in all the other ingredients. Toss around until the carrots are completely coated. Spread out onto a baking tray and cook at the top of the oven for about 40 minutes, until the carrots are browned and tender. Use a spatula halfway through cooking to mix the carrots around a little and add a bit more oil if they seem too dry.

Serve straight out of the oven.

DINNER

STIR FRIED TOFU WITH AUBERGINES

GLUTEN-FREE

Prep time: 10 minutes (including draining time).
Cooking time 16-18 minutes.

Serves 2.

Ingredients:

2 tbsp sesame oil
50g gluten-free flour
1x400g block plain tofu, drained and cut into large squares
A pinch of Sichuan peppercorns, roughly pounded
½ tsp garlic granules
½ tsp Chinese five-spice powder
1 tsp tandoori masala curry powder
½ tsp ground ginger
½ aubergine, cut into large squares
12-14 baby plumb or cherry tomatoes, halved
1 small handful of pine nuts
2 tbsp tamari (gluten-free soy sauce)
2 tbsp sweet chilli sauce (check for gluten-free)

Great food doesn't have to keep you tied to the kitchen for a whole evening. Sometimes you just want to get in and get it done, which is one of the many reasons stir-fries are great. This one is packed with flavour and can be ready to eat in the time it takes you to cook some rice. I use the Cauldron simple tofu for this dish. I leave it to drain for 5 minutes by wrapping it in a clean tea towel and putting a heavy saucepan on top to squeeze out the moisture (you can do this while you're getting your rice ready to save time). Everything is cut quite large for maximum flavour and there is not a great deal of sauce, though neither is it dry. This is a perfect after work dinner with minimal fuss. You do, however, want to dust the tofu pieces with flour before frying to give them a crispy coating. I've used all-purpose gluten-free flour for this, but if you have no gluten issues use whatever flour you have to hand. I promise you this is the only messy part and it's over with quickly. Get cooking, have fun with it and enjoy an easy and exciting meal.

Method

First put the flour into a large bowl and toss the tofu pieces in it until fully coated. Heat half the sesame oil in a wok or large non-stick frying pan and fry the tofu pieces for 6-8 minutes, turning occasionally with tongs, until crisp and browned on all sides. Add the peppercorns, garlic granules, five-spice, curry powder and ginger about 3 minutes before the end of cooking and mix to thoroughly coat. Remove the tofu from the pan and set aside. Rub the pan with kitchen towel and heat the other half of the oil. Fry the aubergine for 4-5 minutes, until soft and browned, then add the cherry tomatoes and pine nuts. Cook for a further 2 minutes until the tomatoes begin to wilt and then add the tamari and sweet chilli sauce. Cook for another two minutes, stirring, until the sauce has mostly gone. Put the tofu pieces back into the pan and stir in. Serve with rice.

Mushrooms with Mung Beans and Sundried Tomatoes

Prep time: 5-8 minutes.
Cooking time: 15 minutes.

Serves 2.

Ingredients:

2 tbsp olive oil
200g mushrooms, quartered
100g sundried tomatoes, sliced
200g cooked mung beans (or one can of green lentils, or black-eyed beans), drained
2 cloves garlic, thickly sliced.
2 tbsp tamari
1 tbsp balsamic vinegar

If you've got cooked mung beans ready to go, then this is a very quick and easy meal to make. If you don't want to cook the beans from dried, then canned green lentils or black-eyed beans are a great substitute, just drain them beforehand. The sundried tomatoes, combined with the thickly-sliced garlic create a truly intense flavour that is balanced wonderfully with the beans and mushrooms. This is a lovely mid-week supper for two.

Method.

Heat the oil in a frying pan or wok and sauté the mushrooms for about 5 minutes, until browned. Add the garlic and tomatoes and fry for another minute, then add the beans. Cook for about 4 or 5 minutes, stirring often, then pour in the tamari and balsamic vinegar. Cook for two more minutes, until most of the liquid has evaporated. Serve with bread or rice.

MUSHROOM AND MANGETOUT RISOTTO

Prep time: 15 minutes.
Cooking time: 30 minutes.

Serves 4.

Ingredients:

2 tbsp olive oil
1 onion, finely diced
2 celery sticks, finely sliced
250g punnet Chestnut mushrooms, quartered
2 cloves garlic, chopped
300g Arborio (risotto) rice
750ml vegetable stock (make sure it's vegan and gluten-free)
150g mangetout
100g vegan cheese, chopped or grated (I used blue cheese style)
A handful of rocket leaves.

A delicious and light summer evening meal that's all done in one pan and doesn't take too long to cook. Risotto is a good option if you want something quick and healthy without too much fuss. This version has chestnut mushrooms and mangetout, with a topping of strong vegan cheese.

Method

Heat the oil in a non-stick pan and sauté the onions and celery together for 2 minutes. Add the quartered mushrooms and cook on a medium heat for 5 minutes. Add the garlic, stir for 30 seconds and then add the uncooked rice.

Fry for two more minutes and then add your vegetable stock, one ladle at a time, allowing the rice to absorb each ladle of liquid before adding the next. Continue this, stirring occasionally, until there are two ladles of stock left and then add the mangetout. Add the last of the stock and cook until the rice is done. You may wish to add a small amount of water if it becomes too dry. Risotto is meant to be quite a moist dish.

At the end of cooking, turn off the heat and add a generous knob of vegan butter, then cover the pan with either a lid or some tin foil. Leave to stand for 5 minutes while the rice absorbs more liquid.

Serve with the vegan cheese and a small amount of rocket leaves.

Green Pea Pasta Bake

GLUTEN-FREE

Prep Time: 30 minutes.
Cooking time: About 1 hour.
Serves 4-6

Ingredients:

2 tbsp olive oil
1 medium red onion, diced
1 medium courgette, diced
6 button mushrooms, quartered
1 head of broccoli, cut into florets
200g green pea pasta, cooked, drained and cooled
2 cloves garlic, chopped
200g cherry tomatoes, halved
1 tbsp vegan and gluten-free Worcester sauce
2 tbsp tamari (make sure it's gluten free)
Salt and pepper to taste
1 batch vegan cheese sauce (page 51)
75g vegan cheese
1 tbsp course cornmeal.

Preheat the oven to gas 6/200C/400F

Heat the oil in a large pan or wok. Add the red onion and fry for 3 minutes, then add the courgette and mushrooms. Cook for another 2 minutes, then add the broccoli and cook for 4 more. Add the garlic and cherry tomatoes and cook for about 6-8 minutes, until the tomatoes are soft. Pour in the Worcester sauce and tamari and give the whole dish another two minutes.

Mix the pasta in with the vegetables, adding salt and pepper as required, and put the whole lot into a suitably-sized oven dish. Pour the cheese sauce over the top and sprinkle on the vegan cheese. Dust the top of the dish with the cornmeal and cook in the middle of the oven for 30-35 minutes, until the top is crisp and browned.

CHICKPEA, APPLE AND CASHEW CUTLETS

GLUTEN-FREE

Preparation time 15 minutes plus cooling time. Cooking time 25 minutes.

Makes 10

Ingredients:

1 can chickpeas
1 can borlotti beans
2 tbsp olive oil
1 tsp cumin seeds
60g cashew nuts
2 cloves garlic, chopped into large pieces
1 small apple, cored and diced
1 onion, diced
1 red pepper, diced
5-6 fresh sage leaves, thinly sliced
1 tbsp ground paprika
2 tbsp lime juice
4 tbsp gram flour
Salt and pepper to taste
More oil for frying.

This is a lightly spiced patty that can be served with a variety of side dishes. I go for a quite simple rice and salad, but you can also put it in some pitta bread or even a burger bun if that's what you have lying around.

Method

First drain the chickpeas and borlotti beans. While they're draining heat the olive oil in a pan and lightly fry the cumin seeds for 30 seconds. Add the cashew nuts and fry for a further minute, being careful not to let them go too dark. Add the garlic and fry for another minute, then add the apple, onion, pepper and sage leaves. Cook for about 10 minutes, or until the apple and vegetables have softened. Add the paprika and fry for another minute or so then turn off the heat. Leave to cool for about 15 minutes.

Preheat the oven to gas 5. Put the drained beans into a food processor, along with the apple and cashew mixture and pulse until blended but still quite chunky. Scrape the mixture into a bowl and add the lime juice, gram flour and salt and pepper. You'll want a fair amount of seasoning for this size mixture, but don't go crazy. Mix well and heat a clean pan with a little oil for frying.

Take two desert spoons and scoop a spoonful of the mixture into the hot pan, using the other spoon to help you. You should be able to fit four of these in at a time. Fry on one side for a few minutes and then flip over. At this point you can flatten the patties a little to make a burger shape. Cook for approximately 8 minutes, flipping them as they get brown. As you finish each batch place them on a baking tray and put them in the oven while the rest are frying. This will not only keep them warm but help seal the edges.

GREEN BEAN AND SPINACH CURRY

GLUTEN-FREE

Prep time: 20 minutes.
Cooking time: About 50 minutes.

Serves 4.

Ingredients:

For the curry sauce:
2 onions, diced
4 cloves garlic, smashed
1 ½ inch piece ginger, peeled and roughly chopped
3 tbsp groundnut oil (or other flavourless oil)
3 tbsp cold water
4 large vine-ripened tomatoes
2 tbsp coconut oil
1 cinnamon stick
2 bay leaves
4 green cardamom pods
1 tbsp coriander seeds
1 tbsp cumin seeds
1 tbsp ground turmeric
1 heaped tsp ground coriander
2 tbsp ground paprika
3 tbsp tandoor masala spice mix (other red spice mixes are also fine)
2 tsp mild chilli powder

Vegans and non-vegans alike will love this curry. This is something you can serve during a family gathering and nobody's going to complain that there's no meat in it. With its full spicy flavour and dark, rich colour, this dish is sure to please any Indian food fan.

The key is to make the sauce separately and use whole spices, then add it to your vegetables towards the end of cooking. The recipe serves four, but even if you're not cooking for that many I'd recommend making a whole batch of the sauce and freezing what you don't use. That way you can have it again at a later time. You will need a blender or food processor to blend the onions and tomatoes. The curry sauce goes well with just about any vegetable you care to cook, so feel free to experiment on your next go around.

Method:

First put the onions, garlic, ginger, groundnut oil and water into blender or food processor and blend until smooth. Spoon out into a dish and set aside. Rinse out the blender and then put the 4 whole tomatoes in. Blend these until smooth and then set aside.

Heat the coconut oil in a large saucepan. Fry the cinnamon stick, bay leaves and cardamom pods for 1 minute, then add the coriander and cumin seeds and fry those for a minute also. Spoon in the onion mixture and cook for about 4-5 minutes, stirring often. Add the rest of the spices and cook for another 2 minutes, then pour in the pureed tomatoes, the cold water and the stock cube.

250 ml cold water
1 veg stock cube (vegan and gluten-free)
Salt and pepper to taste

For the Veg:
2 tbsp coconut oil
400g fresh green beans, toped and tailed (you can also use frozen)
2 sweet peppers, cut into large chunks
1 red onion, large diced
2 red chillies, deseeded and sliced
3 large ripe tomatoes, quartered
Salt and pepper to taste
A handful of coriander leaves, chopped, plus extra for garnish
100ml vegan cream
100g baby spinach leaves, washed

Bring the sauce to the boil and simmer on a gentle heat for 20-25 minutes, stirring from time to time. Season with salt and pepper to taste, turn off the heat and remove the cinnamon stick and bay leaves. Set aside.

Now you want to cook your veg. Heat the coconut oil in a saucepan or wok (a wok is very good for this as long as it's big enough), until quite hot. Put in the green beans, peppers and onions and fry for about 10 minutes, stirring often so that things don't burn. Add the chilli and tomatoes and cook for another 5 minutes or so, until the tomatoes have softened. Season with salt and pepper, then add the curry sauce. Bring to the boil and simmer for 5 minutes. Add the chopped coriander and cream, stir in and heat for another 2 minutes. Add the spinach and fold it in until wilted.

Garnish with more coriander and serve with rice.

ROASTED FENNEL AND BROCCOLI QUICHE

Prep time: About 30 minutes.
Chill time: 1 hour. Cooking
time: 1 hour.

Ingredients:

For the Pastry:
200g soya flour
200g coconut flour (or gluten-free alternative)
1 tsp baking powder
1 tsp salt
2 tsp xanthan gum
150g vegan margarine, plus extra for greasing
150-200ml almond milk (or dairy-free alternative).

For the Filling:
2 fennel bulbs, stalks and base cut off and leaves separated
2 tbsp olive oil
2 cloves garlic, unpeeled
150g cashew nuts, soaked in hot water for 20 minutes, then drained
200g hummus
100ml dairy-free cream
100g plain dairy-free yoghurt
Salt and pepper to taste.
1 large head of broccoli, cut into small florets.

For the Béchamel:
150ml dairy-free cream
75g grated vegan cheese
1 tbsp nutritional yeast.

For this recipe I'm using soya and coconut flour. I've used a fifty percent mixture of each to make a 400g flour mix. The result is a light and crumbly pastry that has a light coconut taste to it. If you don't like the coconut taste, then I would recommend swapping that flour for some other, like rice flour. You can, of course dispense with this part entirely and use a pre-made gluten-free pastry that you can just place into your tart tin. Whichever method you choose, blind baking beforehand produces best results with the pastry. The filling is made by roasting the fennel first with some whole garlic cloves. Cashews and hummus are blended together to make a thick, creamy sauce that sets beautifully when allowed to stand for a short while. I've put the broccoli in raw to give it some bite after cooking. If you prefer your broccoli soft, then you can steam it for 4 minutes before you put it in the quiche. Don't overdo it or you'll end up with mush. A cheese béchamel is poured on top of that to finish it off and then it's given a dusting of paprika prior to cooking.

Method

First make your pastry. Combine the two flours, baking powder, salt and xanthan gum in a mixing bowl and rub in your margarine until you get fine breadcrumbs. Pour in the milk and bring the dough together with your hands. Knead for a minute and then cover and place in the fridge for an hour.

Preheat the oven to gas 6/200C/400F.

Put the fennel and garlic bulbs on a baking tray and drizzle over the olive oil, then use your hands to make sure all the fennel and garlic are covered with the oil. Place at the top of the oven for 15 minutes, until the edges of the fennel start to brown.

Grease a 9 inch, loose bottomed tart tin with margarine and take your pastry out of the fridge. Dust a surface with the soya flour and roll the dough out large enough to cover the tin and sides. It's quite a crumbly pastry, so if you are having trouble at this point then you can place it into the tin a bit at a time and press it down with your fingers. Once you have lined the tin with the pastry, cut a sheet of greaseproof paper and press on top of the pastry, then pour baking beans or dry rice onto the paper. Place in the middle of the oven for 10-15 minutes to cook the pastry.

Once cooked, remove from the oven. Carefully remove the paper with the baking beans and allow to cool.

Turn the oven down to gas 5/190C/375F

Now make the filling. Place the drained cashews, hummus, cream and yoghurt into a blender and puree until smooth. Empty the mixture into a large bowl and season to taste. Discard the garlic from the fennel and place the fennel and the broccoli into the mixing bowl with the pureed mixture. Combine and pour into your pastry crust.

Make the béchamel. Heat the cream in a small pan and add the grated cheese and nutritional yeast. Cook for a few minutes until the cheese is melted and the sauce thickens, then pour over the top of your quiche.

Dust with ground paprika and bake on the bottom of the oven for 45 – 55 minutes, until golden brown and firm. Leave for at least 15 minutes before serving, or chill completely to serve cold.

CREAMED PEARL BARLEY WITH MUSHROOMS, SPINACH AND COURGETTES

Prep time: 15 minutes:
Cooking time: About 50 minutes.

Serves 4.

Ingredients:

1.2 litres vegetable stock (gluten-free)
250g pearl barley, washed and drained
2 tbsp olive oil
150g mushrooms, quartered
1 courgette, diced
2 cloves garlic, chopped
80g baby leaf spinach, washed
2 tbsp nutritional yeast
100ml dairy-free cream
100ml almond milk
¼ tsp ground nutmeg
Salt and pepper to taste.

Pearl barley, in my opinion, is not given anywhere near enough attention. It is a great source of fibre, protein and vitamins. It's very easy to cook (it takes a little longer than rice, but is cooked in a similar way) and has a wonderful flavour. This is a light and creamy vegetable dish that requires the barley to be cooked in a stock until tender. Once it is cooked, the barley should still be quite wet, like a risotto. Just leave it in the pan with the heat off until you are ready to add it to the main recipe.

Method:

Bring the vegetable stock to the boil in a large saucepan. Add the pearl barley and simmer for 35-40 minutes, until most of the stock has gone and the barley is tender. You can add more water if you need to towards the end. The final consistency should be like risotto.

While this is cooking, heat the olive oil in a pan and fry the mushrooms and courgette together for 4-5 minutes, until starting to brown. Add the garlic and fry for another minute, then put in the spinach leaves. Cook for 2 more minutes, until the spinach has wilted, then add the cream and milk, the nutritional yeast and the nutmeg. Bring to the boil, stirring from time to time, then simmer for about 4 minutes to reduce and thicken the sauce.

Once the pearl barley has cooked, spoon it into the sauce and mix in. Season with salt and pepper to taste and serve immediately.

DELICATELY-SPICED PUMPKIN CURRY

GLUTEN-FREE

Prep time: 20 minutes.
Cooking time: 40 minutes.

Serves 3-4

Ingredients:

1 small pumpkin, about 1kg in weight
1 tbsp coconut oil, plus extra as needed
150g frozen whole green beans
100g sliced mushrooms
2 cloves garlic, chopped
1 ½ tbsp hot madras curry powder
1 tsp ground turmeric
1 tsp ginger paste
1 tsp salt
4 tbsp dairy-free yoghurt
1 tbsp tahini
Juice of 1 orange
150ml dairy-free cream
The seeds from 1 pomegranate (optional)
A few coriander leaves to garnish.

The sight of pumpkins on the market shelves always fills me with excitement, which I think is because they're very much a seasonal thing and we only ever see them in the autumn. This recipe uses diced pumpkin in conjunction with orange juice and just a small amount of spices to augment the flavour of the vegetables.

Method

To prepare the pumpkin, first cut the stalk off to create a flat end. Turn the pumpkin onto this end for safety and then cut in half down the middle. Cut those halves in half again to create four quarters. Use a desert spoon to scoop out the seeds and then peel the pumpkin quarters with the knife, making sure you keep the pumpkin on a flat surface. Cut each peeled quarter into three strips and then dice them.

Heat the coconut oil in a non-stick pan and cook the diced pumpkin for 20 minutes on a medium to low heat, stirring occasionally. The pumpkin will soak up the oil so you may need to add a little more part way through the cooking. When the pumpkin is soft most of the way through add the green beans and mushrooms and cook for another 5 minutes. Add the chopped garlic and cook for another minute and then add the spices, the ginger paste, salt, yoghurt and tahini. Allow that to fry for a couple of minutes and then add the orange juice. Stir for a minute more and then pour in the cream. Cook the curry for a few more minutes until you have a thick sauce and the pumpkin is soft all the way through.

Turn off the heat and stir in the pomegranate seeds, if using. Garnish with the coriander leaves and serve with basmati rice.

LENTIL AND PEARL BARLEY STEW

GLUTEN-FREE

Prep time: 20 minutes.
Cooking time: just over 2 hours.

Serves 4-6

Ingredients:

2 tbsp groundnut oil
2 onions, diced
2 carrots, peeled and diced
½ swede, peeled and diced
2 large, ripe tomatoes, diced
1.7 litres veg stock (vegan and gluten-free)
2 tsp English mustard
2 tsp yeast extract
3 tbsp vegan and gluten-free Worcester sauce
1 ¼ cups cooked pearl barley
2 ½ cups cooked green lentils
Salt and pepper to taste

Stews are a bit of an 'anything goes' food. The scope and range of stews are limited only by your imagination. That being said, you still have to make sure you have a good balance of flavours and ingredients that work in harmony with each other. A good stew takes time. I cook mine for at least two hours as you often won't see any changes to it for about 1 ½ hours. My grandmother used to cook hers all day. I used to see my grandfather stirring and seasoning it and for many years thought he was the one who had made it. I was later told that this was incorrect, despite my grandfather claiming all the credit.

I've gone for a very 'British style' stew here, not too dissimilar to the one my grandmother made all those years ago. The lentils and pearl barley help in thickening the stew over time. Towards that last half hour or so of cooking I always go at it with a potato masher. This breaks up the larger pieces and creates a lovely thick consistency.

Method:

Heat the oil in a large, heavy-based saucepan or stew pot. Sweat the onions, carrots and swede, with a lid on, for about 10 minutes, until a little tender. Stir from time to time to make sure nothing sticks. Take the lid off and add the diced tomatoes. Stir in and cook for 5 more minutes. Pour in the stock and bring to the boil, then turn the heat down to a gentle simmer. Add the mustard, yeast extract and Worcester sauce and stir these in. Finally add the barley and lentils. Put the lid back on, so that there is a little gap for some steam to escape, and simmer gently for an hour, stirring occasionally.

Take the lid off and simmer for another hour. You will need to stir more often as the stew thickens to prevent it from sticking to the pan. About 30 minutes before the end of cooking use a potato masher to mash the stew up a little, breaking up some of the larger pieces and thickening the sauce. Season with salt and pepper to taste and serve with rustic bread.

BUTTERNUT SQUASH AND WALNUT WELLINGTON

EASY TO MAKE
GLUTEN-FREE

Prep time: 20 minutes. Cooking time: about 1 hour. Cooling time: 1 hour.

Serves 6

Ingredients:

1 block ready-made puff pastry (or gluten-free alternative), brought up to room temperature
Knob of vegan margarine, for greasing
Dairy-free milk, for basting.

For the squash:
1 small butternut squash, peeled, deseeded and cut into cubes
1-2 tbsp olive oil
½ tsp ground cinnamon
½ tsp ground paprika
3-4 tbsp cold water
Salt and pepper to season

For the béchamel:
1 tbsp vegan margarine
1 tbsp flour (gluten-free if using that option)
200ml dairy-free milk
3 tbsp nutritional yeast
Salt and pepper

1 bag/160g fresh baby spinach
3 tbsp cold water
75g dried apricots, chopped
50g walnut pieces, chopped

This is a substantial main course that has so much flavour your guests will be abandoning their potatoes and asking you for more. This recipe uses butternut squash as a base, which is cooked in paprika and cinnamon to give it a wonderful taste. The squash is layered with spinach, béchamel sauce, dried apricots and walnuts, and encased in puff pastry. Salivating yet? I know I am.

The puff pastry used is ready-made and bought at your local supermarket. I use Jus-Rol, which is vegan. They also do a gluten-free version, for those who are intolerant, making this an extremely versatile dish. The only other gluten in my recipe is in the flour used to thicken the béchamel. You can substitute this for any gluten-free flour and you're good to go. The trick to not getting in a mess with this wellington is to layer it all out in clingfilm first (or whatever eco-friendly version you are using), and use that to mould the filling into a large sausage shape. This is then put in the fridge to chill for an hour before placing onto your rolled-out pastry.

Method

First cook the butternut squash. Heat the olive oil in a pan and add the squash. Cook for 15-20 minutes on a medium-low heat, stirring occasionally until the pieces are soft and can be broken up easily. After 10 minutes of cooking add the paprika, cinnamon and salt and pepper and stir in. You will probably need to add a few tablespoons of water towards the end to help with the cooking and stop it drying out too much. Mash the cooked squash slightly, making sure there are still plenty of lumps, and set aside.

Now make your béchamel. Melt the margarine in a small saucepan and then take the pan off the heat and add the flour. Use a whisk to bring them together. It will immediately form a thick lump at the bottom of the pan. Add the milk, a little at a time, until you get a paste consistency, then put the pan back on the heat and continue adding the milk, whisking as you go to prevent lumps from forming. Add the nutritional yeast and season to taste. Cook on a low heat for about 4 minutes and then set aside. The béchamel will start to thicken as it cools, which is what we want. Just cover it with cling film to stop a skin forming.

Wilt the spinach by cooking it with a few tablespoons of water for about 4 minutes, and then drain in a sieve. Use a spoon to squeeze out as much of the spinach water as you can. Now you are ready to assemble your filling.

Tear off a strip of clingfilm about 18 inches long and place it on your worktop. Spoon the mashed butternut squash onto the film, forming a line about 11 inches long and 4 wide. Spoon the cooled and thickened béchamel sauce on top of the squash, trying not to spill any over the sides. It should be thick enough to do this easily. Use your fingers to spread the spinach out over the top of the béchamel and then sprinkle the apricots and walnuts on top of that. Bring the sides of the clingfilm together, so that the filling becomes sausage-shaped, then twist the ends to seal it. Put this on a plate in the fridge for an hour to cool completely.

Grease a large baking tray and preheat the oven to gas 6/200C/400F.

On a floured surface, roll out your pastry to about 14-15 inches long and 10 inches wide. Place this on the baking tray and then put your chilled filling, upside down, onto the middle of the pastry. Carefully remove the clingfilm without disturbing the filling too much. Now brush all around the visible pastry with the dairy-free milk. Bring the sides of the pastry together, just like you did the clingfilm, and press one on top of the other to seal. Brush any areas with milk that haven't been done. Press down each end and tuck them in, pinching them with your fingers to seal. Now carefully turn the whole thing over so that the sealed bits of pastry are hidden at the bottom. Brush the top with the milk and then gently score diagonal slices only a tiny way into the pastry with a sharp knife. Now score diagonal slices the other way so that you end up with diamond shapes (see picture). Cook towards the bottom of the oven for 30-35 minutes, until the pastry is risen and browned. If you've scored it correctly you'll have raised diamonds on the top. Allow to cool for 10 minutes and then slice into six and serve.

Spaghetti with Coriander and Pea Pesto

EASY TO MAKE
GLUTEN-FREE

Prep time: 20 minutes.
Cooking time: 20 minutes.

Serves 3-4

Ingredients:

For the Pesto:
100g frozen petit pois peas, thawed
60g fresh coriander
40g walnut pieces
Juice of ½ lemon
½ tsp salt
1 ½ tsp garlic puree
150ml cold water.

For the rest:
250g (half packet) dried wholewheat spaghetti (or gluten-free version)
1 tbsp olive oil
1 large aubergine, cut into bite-sized chunks
2 cloves garlic, chopped
100g baby spinach leaves, washed
1 inch of vegan blue-style cheese, chopped very finely.

This pesto has no added oil in it, so it's going to be a whole chunk less calorific than the regular kind. The dish isn't completely oil-free, however, as some is used to cook the aubergines. Aubergine is just one of many possibilities for this pasta. Mushrooms would work very well, as would artichoke hearts or asparagus. Go with what suits you.

Method

First sprinkle salt over the aubergine and set aside in a colander to draw out the moisture, then heat a large pan of boiling water for the spaghetti. While that's coming to the boil, put all the pesto ingredients into a blender and blend until reasonably smooth, then set aside.

Once the pasta water has come to the boil add the spaghetti and boil for 10-12 minutes, stirring occasionally to stop them sticking together. While the pasta is cooking heat the olive oil in a non-stick pan and fry the aubergines for 8-10 minutes. Add the chopped garlic and fry for a further minute and the pour the pesto into the pan. Drain the spaghetti.

Once the pesto mixture has heated through add the baby spinach and stir until slightly wilted. Turn off the heat and then mix in the drained spaghetti.

Serve with the chopped cheese and a couple of leaves of fresh spinach.

Fried Tofu with Chickpeas and Pineapple

GLUTEN-FREE

Prep time: 5 minutes.
Cooking time: 15-20 minutes.

Serves 2.

Ingredients:

2 tbsp sesame oil
1 x 160g pack of pre-cut tofu pieces (or smoked tofu, diced - make sure it's gluten-free)
1 green pepper, diced
1 can drained chickpeas
2 cloves garlic
½ can pineapple chunks, drained, juice reserved
1 tbsp coriander seeds
2 tbsp ground paprika
1 tsp dried oregano
½ tsp ground cumin
8 cherry tomatoes, halved
3 tbsp tamari
4-5 tbsp reserved pineapple juice from the can.

I've used the pre-cut and marinated tofu pieces for this dish. A company called Cauldron sell them, and they are available in most supermarkets. If you can't find them, then smoked tofu will work great here.

Method

Heat the oil in a large frying pan or wok. Add the tofu pieces and the green pepper and fry for 4 minutes, until the tofu becomes slightly crisp. Put in the chickpeas and cook for another 4 minutes, making sure any excess liquid is cooked off. Add the garlic and fry for another minute, then put in the pineapple chunks.

Cook for another two minutes, then add the spices and the cherry tomatoes. Give the dish another two minutes or so, stirring often. Finally add the tamari and the pineapple juice. Cook for 4-6 more minutes, until you have a small amount of thick sauce. Serve with rice.

Three Bean and Sweet Potato Shepherd's Pie

Prep time: 15 minutes.
Cooking time: An hour for the beans after soaking. About 90 minutes for the main dish.

Serves 4-6

Ingredients:

1 ½ cups dried beans (½ cup red kidney, ½ cup black-eyed beans, ½ cup pinto beans), soaked overnight, or a can of each if using canned

For the Sweet potatoes:
2 medium sweet potatoes, skin on, cut into chunks
2 tbsp olive oil
Pinch sea salt

For the Pie Filling:
2 tbsp olive oil
2 celery stalks, sliced
1 red onion, sliced
1 leek, sliced
1 red pepper, diced
1 tsp garlic puree
1 cup dried vegan and

This is a slightly different twist on this classic dish and, for those who are fed up with the standard version, contains absolutely no peas or carrots. A great deal of protein and fibre come from the beans, as well as the sweet potato, which is first roasted with the skin on to give it a fuller flavour.

You can use canned beans, though I have chosen dried. Just add a can of each of the three beans in place of the dried measurements if you are doing that. This will go very well with several of the side dishes in this book, including the broccoli cheese and spiced carrots.

Method:

First drain and wash the soaked beans. Put into a saucepan of water and bring to the boil. Rapid boil for 15 minutes, skimming the scum off the top during this time. Turn down the heat and gently simmer the beans for 50 minutes, until all the beans are tender. You may need to add more water towards the end if it starts to run dry. Drain and rinse at the end. Skip this part if you are using canned beans.

Preheat the oven to gas 7/220C/425F.

Coat the sweet potatoes in the olive oil and the salt and roast in the oven for 35-40 minutes, or until the potatoes are soft and the edges are browned.

While these are roasting make your mashed potato topping by boiling the potatoes for about 10 minutes

gluten-free mince (2 cups frozen mince)
600ml veg stock (vegan and gluten-free)
3 tbsp tamari
1 tbsp yeast extract
Salt and black pepper

For the mashed potato topping:
1kg Marfona or Maris Piper potatoes, peeled and cut into chunks
75g vegan margarine
100ml vegan cream
100ml vegan milk
½ tsp wholegrain mustard (optional)
Salt and pepper to taste

until tender. Drain them and mash using a potato masher. Mix in the margarine, cream, milk and mustard, if using, then season to taste. Cover and set aside.

When the sweet potatoes are cooked, make the pie filling. Heat the olive oil in a saucepan or wok and fry the veg for 5-7 minutes, stirring often. Add the garlic puree and cook for another minute. Add the drained beans, either dried or canned, and cook for another 4 minutes, stirring often. Add the sweet potatoes and the vegan mince, then pour in the veg stock, tamari and yeast extract. Bring to the boil and simmer for about 5-10 minutes, until a lot of the moisture has evaporated. Season with salt and pepper to taste.

Pour the pie filling into a suitably-sized oven dish. Spoon the mashed potato on top and use the back of a spoon to spread the potato out and cover the filling. Drag the tines of a fork across the potato to create a rough surface, and then bake in the middle of the oven for 35-40 minutes, or until browned on top.

COURGETTE TEMPURA WITH CRUSHED NEW POTATOES AND LIME & CHILLI SALSA

GLUTEN-FREE

Prep time: 30-40 minutes. Cooking time: Up to 1 hour.

Serves 4

Ingredients:

For the Salsa:
2 limes, quartered and then each quarter cut into three chunks
1 red pepper, large diced
1 tsp olive oil
1 ½ tsp mild chilli powder
1 tsp salt
1 can chopped tomatoes
2 tbsp tomato puree
130g unrefined sugar
2 tbsp golden syrup.

For the Tempura:
3 Small courgettes, cut in quarters lengthways, and then those quarters halved to create batons
300g gram flour, 100g of which will be used for dusting the courgettes
300ml cold water
1 tbsp salt
4 ice cubes
Enough oil for deep frying
You will also need an additional bowl of cold water to soak the courgettes.

For the crushed potatoes:
1 kg baby new potatoes, cooked until tender and then cooled
2 tbsp olive oil
1 tbsp fresh thyme leaves
Salt to taste.

I've always liked the lime pickle in Indian restaurants, so much so that I keep a jar in the fridge for when I make Indian food and can have a dollop on the side. It's an acquired taste, I know this because no one else in the house eats it apart from me, and even I can only handle a small amount. I think what really draws me to this hot and sour condiment is the fact that it has whole chunks of lime cooked in, like little sour surprises that leap out at you. It is with that in mind that I created this dish, or certainly the salsa part of it. I've used whole chunks of lime cooked down in a tomato sauce with red peppers and plenty of sugar to combat the tartness. I've left the lime pieces in the final dish but feel free to remove them after cooking if you like. The tempura batter is made using gram flour to keep it gluten free, and iced water to ensure that it stays cold. You can use a hand whisk for this batter as it doesn't matter if it's a little bit lumpy. Just get it as smooth as you can before adding the ice.

Method

First make your salsa. Heat the olive oil in a small saucepan and then sauté the limes and peppers for five minutes, stirring occasionally. Add the chilli powder, salt and tomato puree then mix in. Add the can of tomatoes, the sugar and syrup and bring to the boil. Simmer on a low heat for 30 minutes, stirring occasionally, until you have a thick and sweet sauce.

While this is cooking put the courgettes in

the bowl of cold water to soak, then whisk 200g of the gram flour with the 300ml cold water and the salt. Once a batter is formed add the ice cubes. Put the remaining flour into another bowl and set the three bowls next to each other: first the courgettes, then the flour, and then the batter.

For the crushed potatoes, heat the olive oil in a frying pan and put in your new potatoes. Whilst they are cooking use either a fork or a potato masher to break up the potatoes a little, so that they are in small crushed chunks. Don't over mash them. Add the thyme leaves and season with salt to taste. Fry for 7 or 8 minutes, stirring occasionally, until the potatoes are slightly browned.

Heat the deep-frying oil in a medium-sized pan. DO NOT fill the pan more than half full with the oil as it will rise when you put in your tempura. Test that the oil is hot enough by dropping a small amount of the batter into it. The oil will bubble and the batter will rise to the surface when it is ready.

Take 6 to 8 courgette batons from the water and toss them in the gram flour until fully coated. Shake any excess flour off each courgette and place them into the batter until your batch is coated. Take the batter to the frying oil on put in the battered courgettes, one at a time, into the oil. Deep fry for 5 minutes or until the batter is golden, then remove with a slotted spoon and set on some kitchen paper to drain. Repeat this process until all the courgette chunks are cooked.

To serve, place a spoonful of the potatoes in the centre of a plate, stack 2 to 3 courgettes on top of the potatoes and then spoon some of the salsa on the side.

QUICK SAUSAGE AND BEAN CASSEROLE

Prep time: 15 Minutes.
Cooking Time: 30 minutes.

Serves 2

Ingredients:

4 Vegan sausages
3 tbsp groundnut oil
1 red onion, sliced
200g mushrooms, sliced
150g red kidney beans,
cooked and drained
(canned is also fine)
150g black-eyes beans,
cooked and drained
(canned is also fine)
1 tsp chilli powder
1 stock cube
1 tsp wholegrain mustard
1 ½ tsp yeast extract
3 tbsp tomato puree
1 tbsp balsamic vinegar
350ml water

Heat 1 tbsp of the oil in a frying pan and cook the sausages for about 8 minutes, or until browned on all sides. Remove them and cut them into 1 inch lengths, then set aside. In a larger pan, heat the remaining oil and fry the onions and mushrooms for 5 minutes, until mostly cooked. Add the beans, the chilli powder and stock cube and fry for another 2 minutes. Add the mustard, yeast extract, tomato puree, balsamic vinegar and water and bring to the boil. Simmer for 15-20 minutes, until the sauce had thickened and reduced. 4-5 minutes before the end put the cooked sausages back in and cook until fully heated through. Serve with rice, potatoes or bread.

Trade the sausages for gluten-free variety if desired.

Vegan Chilli with Coffee and Chocolate

EASY TO MAKE
GLUTEN-FREE

Cooking time: about 1 hour.
Prep: 20 minutes.

Serves 4.

Ingredients:

2 medium onions, chopped
2 Romano peppers, chopped
3 cloves garlic, chopped
2 tbsp olive oil
1 tbsp chipotle chilli flakes
1 tbsp cumin seeds
1 tbsp dried oregano
2 tbsp dark mild chilli powder
6 tomatoes, roughly chopped
2 tbsp tomato puree
2 vegetable stock cubes
1 can red kidney beans, drained
1 can borlotti beans, drained
2 cans chopped tomatoes
1 can water
1 cup espresso coffee
100g dark chocolate
Juice of 1 lime
400g (1 pack) frozen vegan mince (or 2 cups dried for gluten-free)
Salt to taste

I've been developing this recipe for ages, first when I was a meat eater and now that I'm vegan. This is how it stands at the moment and who knows what changes I might make in the future. This chilli is dark, intense and hot without being overpowering, a great weekend meal. I've made a video of this one on my blog: www.richard-churchphoto.com/blog, so that you can easily follow along. Just search for chilli.

Method

Heat the olive oil in a large saucepan and fry the onions and peppers for five minutes. Add the garlic and fry for another minute.

Grind the whole spices in a pestle and mortar or spice grinder and put these in with the chilli powder and oregano. Stir in and add the fresh tomatoes.

Cook down for five more minutes and then add the tomato puree and vegetable stock. Once those are mixed in put in the beans then the canned tomatoes and the can of water. Add the coffee, chocolate and lime and simmer gently for 40 minutes until a thick sauce is formed.

Add the vegan mince and salt if required and cook for a further 10 minutes. Serve with rice or tortillas.

Vegan Crispy 'Duck' Pancakes

Prep time: 10 minutes.
Cooking time: 15 minutes.

Serves 2

Ingredients:

For the Filling:
1 can braised tofu, drained
1 tsp coconut oil
½ tsp garlic granules
1 tsp Chinese five spice powder
1 tsp mild chilli powder
1 tbsp dark brown sugar
1 tbsp hoisin sauce
2 tbsp dark soy sauce.

For the Pancakes:
6 Chinese pancakes (you can get these from Chinese supermarkets)
6 tsp hoisin sauce
½ cucumber, thinly sliced
4-6 spring onions, thinly sliced.

This is a recipe that I was making even before I became vegan. My wife was vegetarian and I wanted a non-meat version of the dish to serve to her. I use braised tofu for this version, which you can get here, but you can also use wheat gluten. You can actually buy Mock Duck in a can, but I would advise still using these spices to get the flavour.

Try this dish, I think you'll find it pretty close to the real thing. I've made a video of this one, so you can see what to do. Just go to www.richardchurchphoto.com/blog and search for duck.

Method

Thinly slice the tofu so that it has a shredded appearance. Heat the coconut oil in a pan and fry the tofu for 5 minutes, until starting to crisp. Add the garlic granules, fives spice, chilli powder and sugar and stir in. Fry for 2 more minutes and then add the hoisin and soy sauce. Cook for another minute, or until you are left with a thick sauce. Set aside.

Spread a teaspoon of hoisin sauce on one pancake. Put a tablespoon or so of the tofu mixture onto that and then top with some cucumber and spring onions. Roll into a pancake shape and repeat this process until the pancakes are gone. Serve immediately.

MUSHROOM DAHL

GLUTEN-FREE

Prep time: 20 minutes:
Cooking time: Just over an
hour.

Serves 4

Ingredients:

250g yello dahl lentils
1 litre water
2 tbsp coconut oil
1 cinnamon stick
4 cardamom pods
1 tsp cumin seeds
2 small (or one large) red
onions, sliced
250g mushrooms, sliced
3 cloves garlic, chopped
2 tbsp almond butter
100g creamed coconut
2 tsp ground turmeric
2 tsp ground coriander
4 tbsp madras curry pow-
der
600ml veg stock (2 stock
cubes - gluten-free and
vegan)

Wash the lentils until they run clear and put them in a saucepan with the litre of water. Bring to the boil and simmer, with a lid on the pan, for 35-45 minutes, until the lentils are tender. You will need to skim the foam off the top of the water with a spoon as the lentils are cooking. When they are done, strain and set aside.

Heat the coconut oil in a large pan and fry the whole cinnamon stick for about a minute. Add the carda-mom pods and fry for another 30 seconds or so and then add the cumin seeds and fry for an additional 30 seconds. Add the onions and cook for 2 minutes, then add the mushrooms and cook for another 4 minutes. If the mushrooms release too much water, then turn the heat up a little. The water will take a few minutes to evaporate. Add the chopped garlic and fry for an-other minute, then put in the almond butter, creamed coconut and the ground spices. Stir until fully incor-porated, then pour in the veg stock. Bring the stock to the boil, add the dahl lentils and simmer for 15-20 minutes, or until you have a thick curry sauce. Sea-son with salt and pepper if required.

BRAISED TOFU AND BEETROOT SPRING ROLLS

Prep time: 20 minutes.
Cooking time: 25 minutes.

Makes 20-25

Ingredients:

2 tbsp sesame oil
1 can braised tofu, drained and finely sliced
1 medium carrot, peeled and finely julienned (cut into thin strips)
2 cloves garlic, chopped
200g cooked rice
3 tbsp hoisin sauce
2 tbsp tamari
2 tbsp sweet chilli sauce
1 medium beetroot, peeled and grated
20-25 spring roll wrappers
Groundnut, or other flavourless oil for brushing.

The raw beetroot in this dish adds a pleasant earthy flavour to the spring roll that offsets it from the typical spring roll flavours. You can use Chinese pancakes for this recipe as well, but they are not as flexible and do not stretch and bend as well as spring roll wrappers, which makes them easy to split. You can deep fry spring rolls for more even cooking, but oven baking them is a lot healthier.

Method

Preheat the oven to gas 6/200C/400F and brushing a baking tray with oil.

Heat the sesame oil in a non-stick pan, or wok, and fry the tofu and carrots for about 8 minutes, until slightly crisp. Add the garlic and cook for another minute, then add the cooked rice. Cook the mixture for 4 minutes, stirring often to prevent sticking, then pour in the three sauces and continue cooking for another 2 minutes or so, until all the sauce is absorbed.

Put 1 ½ teaspoons of the mix onto a spring roll wrapper and place a teaspoon of grated beetroot on top of that. Roll the wrapper tightly, tucking in the sides, until you have a small triangle left at the end. Wet this with water and stick down to seal. Repeat this until all the filling is used, then place them on the baking tray and brush with oil. Cook in the oven for 15-20 minutes, until golden brown.

Roasted Pumpkin Bolognese

GLUTEN-FREE

Prep time: 20 minutes. Cooking time: about 50 minutes.

Serves 4

Ingredients:

For the Roasted Pumpkin:
500g pumpkin flesh, peeled and cut into wedges (butternut squash is also fine)
2 tbsp olive oil
½ tsp ground cinnamon
½ tsp chilli flakes
Pinch flaked sea salt.

For the Bolognese:
2 tbsp olive oil
1 small onion, roughly chopped
1 red pepper, finely diced
2 cloves garlic, chopped
1 tbsp dried oregano
2 tbsp ground paprika
3 tbsp tomato puree
2 cans chopped tomatoes
2 cans cold water (from the empty tomato cans)
2 veg stock cubes (gluten free and vegan)
2 tbsp balsamic vinegar
1 cup dried gluten-free soya mince, soaked in water for 10 minutes (or 1 ½ cups frozen soya mince).
Salt and black pepper.

This recipe uses the dried gluten-free soya mince mentioned at the beginning of this book. You can use a frozen one just as well, just bear in mind that it might not be gluten free, if that is what you're after. If you're not gluten intolerant, just use the vegan frozen one. The roasted pumpkin adds an alternative taste to this otherwise standard vegan Bolognese recipe. If pumpkins are not out yet, feel free to use butternut squash as a replacement.

Method

Preheat the oven to gas 6/200C/400F.

Put the pumpkin into a mixing bowl and pour over the oil, cinnamon, chilli flakes and sea salt. Rub with your hands until the pumpkin is fully coated, then place on a baking tray in the middle of the oven for 25-30 minutes, until soft and browned. Turn off the oven, chop the pumpkin into pieces about half an inch square, and set aside.

To make the Bolognese, heat the olive oil in a large saucepan, then sauté the onions and peppers for 3-4 minutes. Add the garlic and cook for another minute, then put in the oregano, paprika and tomato puree. Cook for two more minutes and pour in the canned tomatoes. Fill each empty can with cold water and then pour those in too. Add the veg stock and the balsamic vinegar and bring to the boil. Simmer gently for about 20 minutes, stirring occasionally, until you get a reduced tomato sauce. You should have lost about a quarter during this time. Drain the soaked mince, if using, and add that to the sauce. If you're using the frozen mince, then that can go straight in from frozen. Add the chopped, roasted pumpkin and stir it all in. Cook for another 10-15 minutes, season to taste with the salt and pepper and serve with your favourite pasta.

VEGAN SAUSAGES WITH LENTILS

EASY TO MAKE
GLUTEN-FREE

Prep time: 5 minutes.
Cooking time: About 25 minutes.

Serves 3-4

Ingredients:

2 tbsp olive oil
4 vegan sausages, defrosted and cut into chunks
1 red pepper, diced
1 red onion, diced
3 cloves garlic, sliced
3 large, ripe tomatoes, cut into chunks
500g cooked green lentils
3 tbsp tamari
3 tbsp vegan Worcester sauce
1 tsp yeast extract
100ml tomato ketchup
50ml cold water
Salt and pepper to taste

This is another quick and easy dish for mid-week, if you've got some frozen vegan sausages lying around and some green lentils. It's all done in one pan, so there's not a crazy amount of washing up to be done afterwards either. Perfect for the end of a long work day. Defrosting the sausages beforehand makes them easier to cut up. If you're in a hurry you can defrost them in the microwave to speed things up. You can either use any cooked lentils that you have left over from another dish or get them from a can or packet. Use gluten-free vegan sausages, if required.

Method:

Heat the oil in a pan and fry the sausages for about 4 minutes, until starting to brown. Add the pepper and onions and fry for a further 5 minutes, stirring often, then add the garlic and give it 2 more minutes.

Put in the tomatoes and turn up the heat a little. Cook for 5 minutes, until the tomatoes have softened and a lot of the moisture has evaporated, then pour in the lentils and cook on the same high heat for about another 4 minutes.

Add the rest of the ingredients and bring to the boil. Simmer for about 5 minutes or so, until a lot of the liquid has gone, and then serve.

FALAFEL

GLUTEN-FREE

Prep time: 10 minutes.
Cooking time: 16-20 minutes.

Makes 10-12

Ingredients:

2 cans drained chickpeas
¼ tsp salt
Ground black pepper
Handful of mint leaves
Handful of coriander leaves
1 small red onion, diced
2 cloves, garlic, bashed with the flat of a knife
Zest of 1 lime
8 dried apricots, roughly chopped
1 tsp ground cumin
2 tbsp ground paprika
2 tsp ground almonds
2 tbsp gram flour
3 tbsp dairy-free plain yoghurt
Enough groundnut oil for shallow frying.

The falafel you buy in the shops doesn't compare to the stuff you can make at home. In fact, once you start making it yourself, you'll probably never want to buy it again. The combination of fresh herbs, spices and dried apricots, the bite of the lime zest, and the background nutty flavour coming from the ground almonds is a taste sensation. Serve them straight away, or chill them for later. Though they are better right out of the pan, you can reheat them for about 10 minutes in the oven if you are making them in advance.

Method

Put all the ingredients, except for the yoghurt and the oil, into a food processor. Pulse for a few seconds at a time until you get a blended, but still a little chunky, texture. You will need to remove the lid and mix with a spatula a couple of times, so that you're not just turning the bottom of the mixture into a puree. When you've reached the desired consistency, empty it out into a mixing bowl and stir in the yoghurt until thoroughly combined. Test to see if it needs more salt.

Roll the mixture into balls the size of golf balls and set aside on a plate.

Heat about ½ centimetre of oil in a frying pan. Fry the falafel in two batches to not overcrowd the pan, for about 8 minutes. Turn them occasionally with a spoon to make sure that all sides are browned. If serving straight away, keep the first batch warm in the oven, on a low heat, until the second batch is cooked.

SPAGHETTI WITH MUSHROOMS AND CHESTNUTS

EASY TO MAKE GLUTEN-FREE

Prep time: 10 minutes.
Cooking time: 20 minutes.

Serves 2

Ingredients

250g whole wheat spaghetti (or gluten-free alternative)
2 tbsp olive oil
1 medium onion, sliced
250g mushrooms, sliced
180g ready-to-eat chestnuts
2 cloves garlic, chopped
2 tbsp nutritional yeast
1 tbsp plain flour
1 veg stock cube
350ml dairy-free milk
100g vegan cheese, grated
150ml vegan cream
Salt and black pepper.

Bring a saucepan of water to the boil and cook the spaghetti for 10-12 minutes, until al dente. Drain and set aside.

Heat the oil in a pan and sauté the onions for 2-3 minutes, until they start to turn translucent. Turn up the heat a little and add the mushrooms and chestnuts. Fry for another 4 minutes, stirring often, until the mushrooms and chestnuts are browned. Lower the heat again and add the garlic. Fry for 1 minute, then add the nutritional yeast, flour and the stock cube. Mix well and then add the milk, a little at a time, making sure that no lumps form. Bring to a gently simmer and sprinkle in the cheese. You should start to have a thick sauce by this point. Pour in the cream and simmer gently for 2 minutes, stirring often. Season with salt and pepper to taste, then pour over your spaghetti. Stir in and serve with grated vegan cheese on top.

SMOKED TOFU WITH CHICKPEAS AND SATAY SAUCE

GLUTEN-FREE

Prep time: 15 minutes.
Cooking time: 15-20 minutes.

Serves 2

Ingredients:

For the Satay Sauce:
2 tbsp sesame oil
1 tsp garlic puree
100g creamed coconut, crumbled
3 tbsp peanut butter, smooth or chunky (I used smooth)
Juice of ½ lime
3 tbsp tamari
250ml dairy-free milk.

For the Smoked Tofu:
2 tbsp sesame oil
1 pack smoked tofu, diced (make sure they're gluten-free)
1 red onion, sliced
1 carrot, peeled, halved lengthways and sliced diagonally
1 can drained chickpeas
1 tsp garlic puree
1 tbsp flaked almonds
Handful fresh mint, chopped
½ red chilli, thinly sliced.

Smoked tofu is a wonderful addition to any vegan fridge. It's an extra firm, tightly packed block of tofu, marinated to give it a smoky flavour and often coated in sesame seeds and/or almonds. It's perfect for stir fries and other dishes where a lot of movement is involved, due to its ability to hold its shape while cooking. I've made this one with chickpeas and some fresh chilli and mint, as well as doing a satay sauce to go on top. Make sure your canned chickpeas are well drained. The dryer they are, the better they will fry without adding too much moisture to the dish. The satay sauce will thicken as soon as you stop cooking it, so feel free to add a splash of water to loosen it up before serving. Just a splash though, you don't want to impact on the flavour.

Method

To make the satay sauce, first heat the oil in a saucepan, then add the garlic puree and cook for 30 seconds. Add the creamed coconut and peanut butter and cook on a gently heat until you have a liquid consistency. Add the lime juice, the tamari and the milk and bring to the boil. Simmer gently for 4-5 minutes, until you have a thick and creamy sauce.

To make the smoked tofu, heat the oil in a frying pan or wok and saute the tofu for 2-3 minutes, stirring often. Add the onion and carrots and cook for another 4 minutes. Add the chickpeas, turn up the heat a little and cook for another 3 minutes, stirring often. Make sure any remaining liquid has evaporated from the pan, then add the garlic puree, almonds, mint and chilli. Cook for a minute or so more and then serve into bowls, pouring the satay sauce on top.

Spaghetti with Kale, Sundried Tomatoes and Green Olives

Prep time: 5 minutes. Cooking time: 10 minutes.

Serves 2

Ingredients:

250g cooked spaghetti (or gluten-free alternative)

1 tbsp olive oil
50g black kale, finely sliced
100g sundried tomatoes, sliced
80g pitted green olives, whole
1 tsp garlic puree
500ml marinara sauce (page 54)

This is a quick way of using some of the marinara sauce in this book. It's an easy mid-week meal if you've made a batch of the sauce at the weekend. You just put on some spaghetti, throw the ingredients in a pan and add the sauce. You've got an intensly-flavoured meal for two in about 15 minutes.

Method

Heat the oil in a frying pan or wok. Fry the kale, sundried tomatoes and olives for 2-3 minutes, then add the garlic puree, and fry for a minute more. Pour in the marinara sauce, bring to the boil and simmer for 5 minutes, stirring occasionally. Serve with the cooked spaghetti.

WHOLE WHEAT CARAMELISED RED ONION AND MUNG BEAN TART

Prep time: 20-30 minutes.
Cooking time: Just over an hour, plus resting time.
Serves 4

Ingredients:

1 batch whole wheat short-crust pastry (see page 46)
Vegan margarine for greasing
1 batch cheese sauce recipe (see page 51)
200g whole cashews, soaked in cold water for 20 minutes
2 tbsp rapeseed oil
3 red onions, sliced
3-4 tbsp cold water
Salt and pepper
40g soft brown sugar
150g cooked mung beans (see page 45)
Pinch of ground paprika.

Whole wheat pastry is a little heavier than white flour pastry, but it is packed with both flavour and goodness, which is reason enough for giving it a go. I've used flaxseeds as an egg replacer for this to give it an extra fibre boost. The mung beans also contribute immensely, as well as providing a whole host of other nutrients, such as magnesium, thiamine and zinc. I've used the cheese sauce recipe in this book as the filling, along with blended cashews, that have been soaked for 20 minutes to soften them up. The red onions are caramelised with brown sugar, which adds some sweetness to the tart. There's a lot going on in this dish, so I would recommend serving it with a side salad. Something light to balance it out.

Method

Preheat the oven to gas 5/190C/375F and grease a loose-bottomed tart tin with margarine.

Roll out the pastry to just beyond the size of the tart tin and line the tin with it. Line the pastry with greaseproof paper and pour baking beans or uncooked rice into the middle. Blind bake for 15 minutes, remove the paper and beans/rice, then set aside.

Make the cheese sauce recipe.

Heat the oil in a frying pan and fry the sliced onions for about 10 minutes, until brown and soft. Add the 3-4 tbsp cold water to prevent them from drying out too much, then season with the salt and pepper and add the brown sugar. Cook for another 4 minutes, until really soft and caramelised, then turn off the heat and set aside.

Drain the cashews and put all of them, plus half of the cheese sauce into a blender and puree until smooth. Put the onions into a mixing bowl along with the mung beans, add the cashew and cheese sauce mix and stir with a wooden spoon until fully incorporated. Spoon this mixture into the cooked pastry case, then pour the remaining half of the cheese sauce on top. Spread it out evenly with the back of a spoon and sprinkle on the paprika. Cook in the middle of the oven for 30-40 minutes, until golden and set. Let it rest for about 15 minutes before serving.

Baked Tofu with Aubergines and Shitake Mushrooms

Prep time: 15-20 minutes.
Cooking time: About 35 minutes.

Serves 2

Ingredients:

For the Baked Tofu:
1 block firm tofu (the firmer the better), pressed, so that as much moisture as possible has been removed
1 ½ tbsp gram flour
2 tbsp olive oil

For the Aubergines:
2 tbsp sesame oil
1 aubergine, cut into 6 slices, salted and left for 10 minutes to draw out moisture
1 tbsp light brown sugar
2 tbsp tamari

For the Shitake Mushrooms:
1 tbsp sesame oil
120g fresh shitake mushrooms, halved
2 cloves garlic, chopped
3 tbsp cider vinegar
5 tbsp tamari
1 tbsp light brown sugar
1 tsp chilli oil
50ml cold water.

Baking tofu is a great way of getting it crisp without too much fuss. It's also the best way to get larger slices of crispy tofu, as they are not disturbed and broken up during cooking. This dish requires large, flat slabs of crispy tofu, so oven baking it is really the only way to go. I gently dust mine in some gram flour prior to baking and then drizzle olive oil over the top, which is similar to what I would do if I was frying them.

The dryer you can get your tofu the better. Wrap it in a clean tea towel and press it under some weight for about 15 minutes, or even longer if you think you can get more water out. While that's going on you can slice and salt the Aubergines, so that the moisture can be drawing out of those at the same time.

Method:

Preheat the oven to gas 7/220C/425F

Turn the tofu on its side and slice longways through the middle, so that you have two large rectangles. Keep them together and turn the tofu back the way it was, so that the largest surface area is facing up. Cut widthways, again down the middle. You should end up with four rectangular slabs of tofu. Put the gram flour on a plate and gently dust each slice of tofu, without breaking them up, so that they are as coated as possible. Put a small amount of the olive oil onto a baking tray and place the tofu slices on top of that. Drizzle the rest of the oil over the top of the tofu slices and brush to fully coat, remembering the sides as well. Place at the top of the oven and bake for about

30 minutes, or until golden and crisp.

About 10 minutes into the baking, start cooking the aubergines.

Heat the sesame oil in a frying pan and fry the aubergines for about 3 minutes each side. Once both sides are browned and the aubergines soft, sprinkle half of the sugar onto the one side of them, flip them over and cook for another minute. Sprinkle the remaining sugar over the other side and flip them again, giving them another minute. Next, pour the tamari into the pan to deglaze it. Allow the vegetables to soak up the sauce, then remove the aubergines and keep warm.

Now for the mushrooms. Clean the pan if you need to, then heat the tablespoon of sesame oil. Sauté the mushrooms for about 3-5 minutes, until browned. Add the garlic and cook for another minute, stirring often. Add the cider vinegar, tamari, sugar, chilli oil and water and simmer for about 5 more minutes, or until you are left with a small amount of rich, dark sauce. By this time the tofu should be about ready. If not, then keep the mushrooms warm for a little longer.

To serve, stack two slices of crispy baked tofu on top of each other. Arrange the aubergines on top of that and then spoon over the mushrooms.

CORN CHOWDER

GLUTEN-FREE

Prep time: 10 minutes.
Cooking time: About an hour.

Serves 4.

Ingredients:

2 tbsp olive oil
1 onion, finely diced
1 red pepper, deseeded and finely diced
2 cloves garlic, chopped
1 large potato, peeled and diced
2 tbsp gram flour
1.5 litres veg stock (gluten-free and vegan)
1/3 cup dried pearl barley, washed and drained
2 tbsp Dijon mustard
1 ½ cups frozen or canned sweetcorn
100ml vegan cream
Salt and pepper to taste

I like my corn chowder to be a filling main course, so you will see that this recipe is packet with stodgy goodness. Add a couple of crusty bread rolls and you've got a perfect evening meal that will warm you right through. Make sure you dice the potatoes small, so that they cook more quickly and thicken the soup by the time it's ready. Use a potato masher to break them up further towards the end, but do this gently so as not to mash up the rest of the ingredients.

Method:

Heat the oil in a large saucepan and fry the onions and peppers together for 5 minutes, stirring often. Add the garlic and fry for another minute, then add the diced potato. Cook for another minute or so and keep stirring to prevent the potatoes from sticking. Add the gram flour and mix in thoroughly, then pour in the veg stock, a little at a time, adding more as the sauce thickens. Keep stirring throughout. Bring the stock to the boil, then add the pearl barley, Dijon mustard and sweetcorn. Partially cover the soup with a lid and simmer for 40-45 minutes, stirring from time to time to prevent sticking.

When the time is up take off the lid and mash the potatoes slightly with a masher. Simmer with the lid off for another 10-15 minutes, then add the vegan cream. Stir to combine, bring back up the heat but do not boil it. Season with salt and pepper to taste and serve immediately.

DESSERTS

AQUAFABA CHOCOLATE MOUSSE

GLUTEN-FREE

Prep time: 25 minutes.
Chilling time: 2 hours.

Serves 4.

Ingredients:

For the aquafaba:
Water from 2 cans chickpeas (about 350ml), strained into a saucepan
1 tsp cream of tartar
4 tbsp castor sugar

For the Chocolate mix:
150g dark dairy-free chocolate, melted
50g vegan margarine, melted
1 tsp vanilla extract
2 tbsp castor sugar.

Aquafaba, if you don't already know, is the water produced from cooking chickpeas. In the canned version it is the water the beans are stored in. When whisked, the water begins to foam and then slowly becomes white and stiff, just like egg whites. Aquafaba can be tricky in the beginning, but a little practice will get you there in no time.

This dish is almost identical to the classic method of making chocolate mousse, in that the chocolate is melted and then folded in with the aquafaba. With the classic way you would mix the egg yolks in with the chocolate before doing this to thicken and enrich them. I do this with vegan margarine and vanilla extract to get as close to an emulsification as possible. Technique here (and, in fact, throughout this recipe) is crucial. Rather than pouring the whole chocolate mix into the aquafaba, it is important to first bring a couple of spoonfuls of the aquafaba to the chocolate and stir that in. This loosens the chocolate to allow for a better amalgamation, without losing all the air from the chickpea water you just spent ten minutes whipping. Once that is done, you then add that mixture to the aquafaba and gently fold it in with a spatula.

If you haven't tried this kind of vegan cooking before, please don't be put off. The sense of achievement when you pull a couple of beautiful and light mousses from the refrigerator is immense, and worth every minute you put into making them.

Method

First you want to reduce your chickpea water by one third. Bring the water to the boil in the saucepan and simmer for about 5 minutes until you can see that it has reduced in volume by approximately one third (you can do this more accurately by measuring before and after cooking in a measuring jug – you'll want to lose about 100ml). Allow the water to cool completely. I do this by pouring it into a jug and then putting the jug on iced water to speed up the process.

Once it is cool you can begin making your aquafaba. Pour the chickpea water into a clean mixing bowl (make sure it is free of any grease) and add the cream of tartar. Put your electric whisk on a medium setting and begin whisking the water. Do this for about 4 minutes. The water will first become foamy and then start to whiten and thicken. You need to be patient here if you haven't done it before, but it will gradually happen. The aquafaba should now be at the soft peak stage, where the peaks you make sink back a little. Now turn the electric whisk up a bit and beat for another 3 minutes, until the peaks are stiffer. At this stage add your sugar and whisk for another 3-5 minutes to get to the stiff peak stage. Peaks will stay where they are, and you'll be able to turn the bowl upside down without any movement from the aquafaba. Remove the whisk and set aside.

During the whisking process melt your chocolate and margarine so that they are cooled slightly by the time the aquafaba is ready. Mix the chocolate, margarine, sugar and vanilla together until you have a smooth consistency. Now add, a spoonful at a time, one third of the aquafaba to the chocolate mix. Stir until you get a smooth, loose blend. Once this is done, pour the chocolate mixture into the remaining aquafaba and fold gently using a large spoon or spatula, until you have a light chocolate foam. Spoon this into your serving dishes and place in the fridge for at least 2 hours. To serve, dust with cocoa powder and garnish with a sprig of mint.

POACHED PEARS WITH BLUEBERRY COMPOTE

GLUTEN-FREE

Prep time: 15 minutes.
Cooking time: 25 minutes.
Cooling time: 3 hours or overnight

Makes 6 Pears.

Ingredients:

For the Poached Pears

6 pears, peeled with stalks still on
1 Litre apple juice
500ml cold water
250g sugar

For the blueberry compote

350g frozen blueberries (fresh is also fine)
150g sugar
2 tbsp lemon juice.

These pears are better if you eat them the day after you make them. There, now I've said it, you can feel free to ignore me. Nobody will judge you here.

At the very least you want to let it all go cold, so a couple of hours in the fridge is a must. Chilling time aside, poached pears are easy to cook and make you look like a diva in the kitchen.

Method

Pour the apple juice and water into a deep saucepan big enough to fit your 6 pears. Bring the liquid to a gently simmer and then pour in the sugar. Stir and simmer for 5 minutes to allow the sugar to dissolve then gently place in your pears. Be very careful not to let the liquid splash as it will burn. Gently simmer the pears for 25 minutes or until you can put a sharp knife into one and it feels soft.

While the pears are simmering, place the blueberries, sugar and lemon juice into a smaller pan and bring these to a gentle simmer. Cook for 15-20 minutes, stirring occasionally, until the compote easily coats the back of a spoon. Once done, remove from the heat and allow to cool in the pan.

As soon as the pears are cooked, turn off the heat and allow these also to cool, still in their syrup, in the pan. It will be about an hour before you can put them in the fridge. When everything is cool enough, transfer to suitable containers and store in the fridge for at least a couple of hours but preferably overnight. To serve, stand a pear upright on a small plate and spoon some compote over the side. You can also add a little vegan cream with these if you like.

211

FOREST FRUIT CHOCOLATE CAKE

Prep time: 30 minutes. Cooking time: 1 hour 15 minutes, plus cooling time.

Makes 1 cake

Ingredients:

For the cake mix:
1 tbsp chia seeds
4 tbsp cold water
400g vegan margarine, softened
400g unrefined castor sugar
1 tsp vanilla extract
400g buckwheat flour
1 tsp salt
1 tsp gluten-free baking powder
50g cocoa powder
100g dark chocolate, melted
250g frozen forest fruits, thawed and drained with as much moisture squeezed out as possible (reserve the liquid for the filling)
50ml almond milk

For the compote filling:
250g frozen forest fruits, thawed. Liquid reserved.
150g sugar

For the cake topping:
200g dark chocolate, melted
50g vegan margarine
150ml vegan cream
50g grated dark chocolate
1 tbsp icing sugar.

Love forest fruits? Love chocolate? I'm right with you.

Combining these two great ingredients is something I've wanted to try for a while. There's something very dark and earthy about it; a slight bitterness to the fruit that is deeply pleasant in combination with its indulgent chocolate surroundings. Harmonious, yet contrasting enough to arouse the pallet's interest. This is a cake for the cooler seasons; something to cosy up to as the nights draw in and the air outside becomes crisp and damp. Due to the wet fruit content, this cake needs to be cooked a little longer than some others, and it is best to cover it so that the top doesn't burn and dry out. For that I have used greaseproof paper and tin foil to act as a lid. This is done for the first hour, before removing for the last 15 or 20 minutes of cooking.

Method

Preheat the oven to gas 4/180C/350F and grease two 9 inch, loose-bottomed cake tins. Line the bottom of the tins with greaseproof paper. Make a second circle of greaseproof paper for the top of each tin and do the same with tin foil. You should have 6 rounds in total, 4 greaseproof and 2 tin foil.

First make the cake mix. Put the chia seeds and the cold water together in a small bowl and leave for 10 minutes until it becomes a thick and gloopy mixture.

Put the margarine and castor sugar into a mixing bowl and cream with an electric whisk until you have a light, fluffy mixture. Once this is done mix in the chia seeds and the vanilla extract. In a separate bowl sift the flour, salt, baking powder and cocoa powder together and then add to the wet cake mixture. Stir with a wooden spoon until fully combined. Make sure your melted chocolate has cooled and then add it to the cake mixture along with the thawed fruit and almond milk. Mix thoroughly.

Divide the mixture between the two cake tins, then put the greaseproof paper lids onto each, followed by the tin foil lids. Cook in the bottom of the oven for 1 hour, then remove the lids and cook for another 15 minutes or so, until an inserted toothpick comes out clean.

While the cakes are cooking make your compote. Put the 250g of forest fruit, plus any draining liquid you have left over from thawing. Add the sugar and bring to the boil. Turn down the heat and simmer, stirring occasionally for 15 minutes until it has a thick, jam-like consistency. Set aside to cool.

Once your cakes are cooked, take them out of the oven and leave them in their tins for 10 minutes, then turn them out onto a cooling rack. Leave to cool for about an hour.

When you are ready to assemble the cake make the topping. Remember that it will set quickly so only make it when you are ready to put it on the cake. In a bowl, mix the melted chocolate with the vegan margarine and leave to cool for a few minutes. Once it is cool to the touch, whisk in your cream. It will start to thicken immediately.

To assemble the cake, spread your compote onto the top of one cake and then place the other cake on top of that. Spoon the chocolate topping on top of the assembled cake and use a pallet knife to spread it over the top and sides. Unless you're a dab hand this will be tricky, but try to get it as even as you can. Leave to set for 10 minutes and then sprinkle the grated chocolate over the top. Dust with icing sugar when you are ready to serve. You can add some frozen fruit for decoration here if you like as well.

MANGO SLICE

GLUTEN-FREE

Prep time: 30 minutes.
Cooking time: 5-7 minutes. Chilling and setting time: at least 4 hours.

Makes 12 squares.

Ingredients:

For the base:
1 batch Homemade
Granola recipe (page 77)
150g pitted dried dates.
75g vegan margarine,
melted, plus a little extra
for greasing

For the filling:
150g cashew nuts, soaked
overnight and drained
2 cans coconut milk
1 mango, peeled and diced
200g sugar
1 ½ tsp agar agar powder
1 tsp vanilla extract

For the topping:
1 mango, peeled and diced
1 apple, cored, peeled and
diced
Juice of 1 lemon
100ml cold water
250g sugar

This dessert might be a little bit involved, but it really is worth the effort. It's basically a granola base, with a set mango and coconut filling and topped with a smooth mango jelly. It looks fantastic on the plate and will impress the hell out of your dinner guests. Thanks to the agar agar, the filling sets very quickly, so it can be made the same day you want to eat it. However, I would recommend starting early if you want it for that evening. You can set it entirely in the fridge if you have the space, but I have chosen the freezer to speed things up a bit. You can then either leave it in the freezer and thaw before serving, or you can store it in the fridge once it has set. The mango topping has a tendency to slide off once it has been cut, so I would recommend scoring the filling with a fork before pouring the topping on. This will give it a rough surface to cling to once it has set.

Method:

Grease a deep, square oven dish with some margarine.

First you want to make the base. Put the granola and the dates into a food processor and blitz until you have a gooey, crumbly mixture. Put this into a mixing bowl and add the margarine. Mix this together and press it down into the oven dish, so that it completely covers the bottom and is about a centimetre deep. Put it in the freezer to chill for an hour.

While the base is setting you can make the filling. Put all the filling ingredients into a blender and puree until completely smooth. Pour the mixture into a saucepan and bring to a gentle simmer, stirring often to prevent sticking. Simmer gently for 5-7 minutes, continuing to stir. Take off the heat and cover with cling film to prevent a skin forming, and then leave to cool. Pour the cooled mixture onto the granola base, making sure that it spreads evenly, then leave to set in the freezer for about two hours. It will have a firm blancmange-like consistency when it is ready.

Once it is set you can make the mango topping. Put all the ingredients into a saucepan and bring to the boil. Simmer gently for about 20 minutes, until you have a thick sauce that easily coats the back of a spoon. Allow to cool for about 15 minutes and then puree in a blender.

Score the top of the set filling slightly with a fork and then pour the mango topping over it, spreading it out evenly with the back of a spoon. Leave to set for another hour or so. Once it is completely set, cut the dessert into 12 even squares. From here you can either leave it in the freezer or transfer it to the fridge prior to serving. If freezing completely, allow an hour or so to thaw before serving.

CHOCOLATE TART

GLUTEN-FREE

Prep time: Up to one hour.
Cooking time: 25 minutes.
Chilling time: 3 hours or overnight.

Ingredients:

For the base:
300g buckwheat flour
150g vegan margarine, plus extra for greasing
1tsp salt
1tsp baking powder
60g cashew nuts
100g dates
50g dark muscovado sugar
4 tbsp almond milk.

For the Filling:
1 x 400g pack of plain tofu, drained
200ml dairy free single cream
50g ground almonds
90g dark muscovado sugar
50g coco powder
75g vegan margarine, softened
200g dark, dairy-free chocolate such as Green & Blacks, melted.

For the topping:
100g of the same dark chocolate as the filling, melted
50g vegan margarine, melted
50ml dairy-free single cream.

I think chocolate is one of the main reasons many vegetarians wince at the thought of going the full hog and switching to veganism. And I get it: chocolate is amazing. I certainly wouldn't want to live without it. Hopefully this recipe will help change some minds about chocolate, because it really doesn't have to have dairy to be delicious. I also use buckwheat flour to keep this desert gluten free, but it does contain nuts.

Method

To make the base, put the flour, salt and baking powder into a bowl and add the margarine in small pieces. Rub with your fingertips until the mixture resembles breadcrumbs. Blend the cashew nuts in a high-quality blender and add to the mixture. Blend the dates separately and add those as well, then add the sugar. Mix these ingredients together and then pour in the almond milk. Bring it all together with your hands and knead into a dough. Cover with cling film and leave in the fridge for an hour.

Preheat the oven to gas 5/190 C/375 F

Take the pastry dough out of the fridge and roll it out using the buckwheat flour to stop it sticking. Grease a 10-inch pie tin with some of the vegan margarine and line it with the pastry. Don't worry if it breaks up, just press it into the base of the tin and up around the edges with your fingers. You'll have some pastry left over so feel free to chill this for something else. Once the tin is lined, cut a square of greaseproof paper and press it down on top of the pastry and cut away any edges that stick up too much. Fill the paper with raw rice or baking beans and bake in the bottom of the oven for 15 minutes. Remove the rice and greaseproof paper and bake for a further 10 minutes. Leave to completely cool.

To make the filling, blend all of the filling ingredients together until completely smooth. You will have to stop repeatedly to scrape down the sides with a spatula. If the mixture is too stiff then you can add more cream to loosen it. You are looking for a consistency similar to cake mix

Once the tart base is cooled, pour in the filling, spreading it to the edges. Cover with cling film and chill in the fridge for at least 2 hours, or overnight if you like.

An hour before serving the tart, remove it from the fridge and make the topping.
Mix together the melted chocolate and margarine until completely smooth. Allow to cool slightly and then add the cream. Stir with a whisk to thoroughly combine and then, using a spoon, spread the topping over the tart. Leave to set outside of the fridge for an hour. Slice and serve.

CREPE SUZETTE

Prep time: 15 minutes:
Cooking time: About 4 minutes per pancake.

Serves 4

Ingredients:

For the Pancake Batter:
250g self-raising flour
½ tsp salt
1 tsp baking powder
25g unrefined sugar
750-800ml dairy-free milk
(I used almond)
Oil for frying

For the Orange Syrup:
100g soft brown sugar
Juice and zest of 2 oranges
1 tsp vanilla extract
60g vegan margarine
100ml dairy-free cream

This is a vegan version of the French dish, which is essentially pancakes with orange syrup. The crepes and sauce can be cooked in advance and then heated together when it is time to serve. If you are serving straight away, then it is better to keep the crepes warm in a low oven. When it is time you can put the folded pancakes back into a frying pan and pour some of the sauce into the pan. Traditionally, the sauce would contain alcohol, which you could flambé at the last moment (always impressive in front of guests) but, as I don't drink, I have made it without.

If you've never tried these, they are certainly worth having a go at. Folding the pancakes into quarters while they're in the pan might be tricky at first, but you'll soon get the hang of it. If you're not confident in doing this you can always fold them afterwards, once they've cooled a bit.

Method:

First make the pancake batter. Put all the dry ingredients into a mixing bowl and slowly add the milk, whisking as you go to avoid any lumps forming. You can do this in a food processor or blender if you prefer.

Next make the syrup. Melt the sugar in a saucepan, stirring from time to time, and then add the orange juice and zest. Let it simmer for a minute, then add the vanilla and margarine. Simmer for about 2-3 more minutes. Take the pan off the heat, leave for a minute and then add the cream. Whisk in thoroughly and set aside until needed.

To make the pancakes, heat a tablespoon of oil in a non-stick frying pan until quite hot. Pour just under a ladleful of the batter around the edge of the pan, then tip the pan slightly in a circular motion to spread the batter around the base. Allow to cook for about 2 minutes before trying to move it, then slide a spatula underneath the pancake to loosen it. If it starts to fall apart, then it is probably not cooked enough on that side, so cook for a bit longer. Gently turn the pancake over with the spatula and cook the other side for the same amount of time. You want it just browned and not too crisp. Once it is done, fold the pancake in half, and then in half again, so that you have a quarter circle of folded pancake. Put the pancake onto a tray and either keep warm in a low oven or set aside to reheat later.

Repeat this until all the batter has gone (about 8-10 pancakes). Once you have the folded pancakes you can start cooking to order. Heat the pan back up, using a tiny bit of oil if needed, and place two of the pancakes into the pan. Reheat on both sides and then pour 2-3 tablespoons of the sauce into the pan with the pancakes. Allow it to bubble, and turn the pancakes once to fully coat them. Serve onto a warm plate and continue until all the pancakes are gone.

DOUBLE CHOCOLATE & PECAN COOKIES

Prep time: 15 minutes.
Cooking time: 15 minutes, plus a short amount of cooling time.

Makes about 24

Ingredients:

Wet:
300g unrefined sugar
300g vegan margarine
1 tsp vanilla extract

Dry:
300g general purpose gluten-free flour
1 tsp xanthan gum
½ tsp salt
100g cocoa powder
1 ½ tsp bicarbonate of soda
100g dairy-free dark chocolate, chopped into small pieces
75g chopped pecans
100ml dairy-free milk

These cookies are dark and rich, soft inside with a crisp outer coating. The essence of what a cookie should be, with the added benefit of being both vegan and gluten-free. The pecan nuts add an extra depth and crunch, something that appeals to me. If you have a nut allergy, these can be made without them. Just leave them out of the recipe. I've used a general-purpose gluten-free flour, but buckwheat also works well. Indeed, so does regular flour if you have no problems with wheat (you can leave out the xanthan gum if using regular flour). A firmer dough is better for a crunchier biscuit, as opposed to a batter that you would spoon onto a baking tray before cooking. The dough is rolled into balls about the size of a Brussels sprout, and then flattened slightly with the palm of the hand. This is so that they will form the cookie shape as, without doing so, the cookies will come out too thick and a little more like cakes.

They are quick and easy to make and only take 15 minutes in the oven, so they're great to make on a weekend morning for the kids (or even just for yourself). Give them a try, I think you'll be pleased with the results.

Method:

Preheat the oven to gas 4/180C/350F and line a large baking sheet with greaseproof paper.

Put the sugar and margarine together in a large mixing bowl and whisk with an electric whisk until you have a light and fluffy mixture. Add the vanilla extract and then whisk for another minute until fully combined. In a separate bowl, sift the flour, xanthan gum, salt, bicarb of soda and cocoa powder together, and then stir in the chocolate and nuts. Add the margarine mixture to the flour mixture, then pour in the dairy-free milk. Bring it all together with your hands to form a sticky brown dough.

Take a spoonful of the dough and roll into a ball, roughly the size of a Brussels sprout, and place it on the baking tray. Repeat the process until you fill up the tray, leaving about 1 ½ inches of space around each dough ball to allow them to spread. Flatten each ball to about a centimetre thick with the palm of your hand and then place near the top of the oven for 15 minutes, or until crisp on the outside. Remove from the oven and leave them to cool on the tray for a few minutes before transferring to a cooling rack. Load up the next tray and do the same all over again, until all of the cookie dough is gone.

COFFEE & WALNUT BROWNIES

Prep time: 15 minutes.
Cooking time: 25 minutes.
Cooling time: 2 hours

Makes 12

Ingredients:

For the Brownie

300g self-raising flour
50g cocoa powder
½ tsp salt
1 tsp baking powder
1 tbsp ground flaxseeds
150g unrefined sugar
60g vegan margarine, room temperature, plus extra for greasing
150 ml espresso coffee (or instant, if that's what you have)
150ml dairy-free milk (I used rice milk)
1 tsp vanilla extract
170g dark, dairy-free chocolate, melted
70g chopped walnuts

For the Topping

100g dark, dairy-free chocolate, melted
50g vegan margarine
40g chopped walnuts

I used to make brownies every day in one restaurant I worked. It was a constant routine, almost as soon as I made them they would be sold, and I would have to make some more. After three years of that I was making brownies in my sleep.

This recipe is quite a bit different from that one. For one thing it's vegan, but also it veers from the basic brownie recipe by the addition of chopped walnuts and espresso coffee. The coffee haters out there need not worry. It adds more depth than it does coffee flavour. If you really can't be persuaded, then simply exchange the coffee for more dairy-free milk, which will give you the same liquid content. I do urge you to try it with the espresso, though, as it adds something quite special to the mix. This brownie has a chocolate topping, made with vegan margarine and melted chocolate, and chopped walnuts are sprinkled over that while it is still wet.

Method:

Preheat the oven to gas 4/180C/350F, then grease a 12 x 9 inch baking tray and line it with greaseproof paper.

Sift the flour and cocoa powder into a large mixing bowl. Add the salt, baking powder, flaxseeds and sugar and mix together. Stir in the margarine and then add the espresso, milk and vanilla extract. Use a whisk to thoroughly combine all the ingredients into a smooth batter. Add the melted chocolate and walnuts and whisk again. Pour or spoon out the mixture onto the baking tray and flatten it out with a spatula. As the melted chocolate cools this will become slightly more difficult because the mixture will thicken. Place the tray in the middle of the oven and cook for 20-25 minutes, until cooked but still a little moist in the middle.

Once cooked, turn the tray out onto a large chopping board. The tray should lift easily off the brownie. Remove the greaseproof paper and allow to cool for an hour.

Once the brownie is cool, melt the topping chocolate and whisk in the vegan margarine. Spread over the top of the brownie with a pallet knife and then sprinkle the chopped walnuts on top. Leave to cool for another hour, then cut into 12 pieces.

BUCKWHEAT CHERRY PIE

GLUTEN-FREE

Prep time: 15-20 minutes.
Chilling time: 1 hour.
Cooking time: about 45
minutes.

Serves 6-8

Ingredients:

2x 500g packs frozen cherries
250g unrefined sugar
2 tsp vanilla extract
Vegan margarine for greasing
1 batch buckwheat shortcrust pastry (page 47), chilled
Gluten-free flour for rolling
Dairy-free milk for brushing

I should have put this in the breakfast section, because my favourite breakfast is a cold slice of yesterday's fruit pie with a dash of vegan cream. I go nuts for it. Of course, I don't actually have it that often because I'm not making pies every day. When I do make them, however, it's always the next morning I'm looking forward to.

I've used frozen cherries for this pie, as it removes all the arduous work during prep. They produce a fair amount of liquid, so it's a good idea to cook them down a little with the sugar first, then use a slotted spoon to put the cooked cherries into the pie base. You can always add more of the remaining liquid from the pan if it's looking too dry. Blind baking is also essential, as it is with so many shortcrust pies, to make sure you have a firm and cooked base before adding the wet filling.

Method:

Put the cherries, sugar and vanilla into a saucepan and bring to the boil, stirring from time to time while it heats up. Reduce the heat and simmer for 20-30 minutes, until the cherries are soft and the sauce is reduced.

Preheat the oven to gas6/200C/400F and grease a deep pie dish with the margarine.

While the cherries are cooking, roll out 2/3 of the pastry dough on a floured surface, until it exceeds the size of the pie dish with enough to cover the sides. Gently place the pastry into the dish (you can press down any cracks that appear while doing this), and trim away the excess.

Next, line the dish with greaseproof paper, so that the paper sits on top of the pastry, then fill the dish with dried rice or baking beans. Bake the pastry in the oven for 10 minutes, then remove the rice and paper and bake for another 5 minutes, so that the base is firm and slightly cooked.

Once the cherries are done, use a slotted spoon to remove them from the sauce and fill the pie with them. You can add a bit of the remaining liquid here to give the filling some moisture.

Roll out the other third of the pastry to the size of the pie dish and gently place over the top, trimming any excess. Press down the edges with the tines of a fork and then brush over the surface with dairy-free milk. Put two slits in the centre of the pie lid to allow steam to escape during cooking, then put the pie in the middle of the oven. Bake for 25 minutes, or until golden brown, and allow the pie to cool slightly before serving.

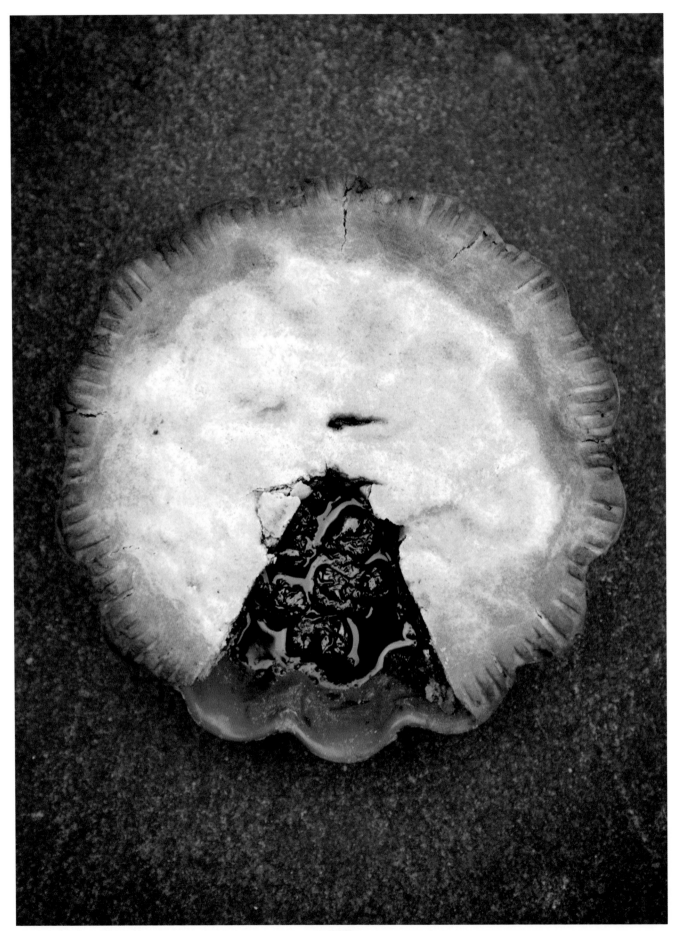

SEMOLINA PUDDING

Prep time: 5 minutes.
Cooking time: 15-20 minutes.

Serves 4.

Ingredients:

1 litre rice milk, plus extra if needed
200ml vegan cream
150g coarse Semolina
150g unrefined sugar
½ tsp ground cinnamon
¼ tsp ground allspice
¼ tsp ground nutmeg
1 tsp vanilla extract
Zest of 1 lemon
4 tbsp maple syrup

When I was in school, this dessert was the highlight of my week. After growing up I had forgotten all about it, then a few years ago I got a real sudden craving for semolina pudding. I had been seeing semolina flour in the supermarket but never actually buying any, and at some point it must have triggered that memory, because from then on I was determined that I was going to have some. I learned how to make it before I became vegan, and then later adapted it to the vegan diet.

If you haven't tried semolina pudding before, then think of it as sort of a cross between polenta and rice pudding. It's a deliciously sweet and creamy dessert, yet very simple in appearance. Just like polenta, it thickens very quickly as it cools, so it is better to serve it as soon as it is made. You can make it in advance, but you will have to add more liquid when you heat it back up again.

Method:

Put the milk and cream in a large saucepan and bring to the boil. Use a whisk to create a whirlpool in the milk/cream mixture and then gently pour in the semolina, continuing to whisk as you do so to prevent lumps from forming. The mixture will start to thick quite quickly. Add the sugar and keep stirring, and when the mixture starts to bubble, turn the heat down to a gentle simmer.

Put in the spices, vanilla extract and lemon zest and whisk again to incorporate. Add the maple syrup and simmer very gently for about 10 minutes, whisking often. If it becomes too thick you can always add more milk to thin it out.

Serve immediately either on its own, or with some cubes of dairy-free chocolate mixed in.

CHOCOLATE CHEESECAKE WITH RASPBERRY TOPPING

EASY TO MAKE
GLUTEN-FREE

Prep time: 20 minutes.
Cooking time: 15-20 minutes. Chilling time: 2-3
hours.
Makes 4

Ingredients:

For the base:
150g (half packet) oat biscuits. Check ingredients as
some are vegan and some
are not.
30g vegan margarine,
melted.

For the Cheesecake Filling:
350g silken tofu
100g creamed coconut
100ml vegan cream
60g soft, white vegan
cheese
100g sugar
1 tsp vanilla extract
100g dark chocolate

For the Topping:
300g fresh raspberries
200g sugar

This is a really decedent dessert that takes a little bit of
time to make but the results are well worth it. This recipe
is easily made gluten-free, just swap the biscuit base for a
gluten-free alternative. You may need to add some sugar as
some gluten-free biscuits are not as sweet.

Method:

First make your base. Crush the biscuits in a bowl. You can
do this with a food processor if you like but I use a rolling
pin. Once they are like rough breadcrumbs mix in your
melted butter until thoroughly combined. Select four glass
desert dishes and put a quarter of the base into each one,
pressing down with your fingers or a spoon to compress
them. Put the glasses in the fridge and chill for half an hour.

Next put all your filling ingredients, except for the chocolate, into a blender and puree until the mixture is smooth.
Break the chocolate up into small pieces. Heat it in a bowl
in the microwave for about a minute, or until it is partially
melted. Stir the chocolate pieces for a few minutes while the
rest of it melts. Allow to cool for 5 minutes and then pour
into the cheesecake mixture. Puree once more. Pour this
mixture into the glass bowls on top of your biscuit base,
remembering to leave a small amount of space for the topping. Place the glasses back in the fridge for 2 hours.

In the meantime, put your raspberries and sugar into a pan
and heat until it starts to bubble. Simmer gently for 15-20
minutes until a thick jam-like consistency is formed. Turn
off the heat and leave to cool for a couple of minutes. Pass
the raspberries through a strainer to remove the seeds. You
can leave a few in if you like for aesthetics, but trust me,
you don't want to be spending your dessert time picking
seeds out of your teeth! Leave the jam to cool and then
spoon on top of the cheesecake. Chill for one more hour
and you are good to go.

DOUBLE CHOCOLATE MUFFINS

GLUTEN-FREE

Prep time: 20 minutes (including standing time).
Cooking time: 25 minutes.

Makes 12 Muffins

Ingredients:

1 tbsp chia seeds
3tbsp water
300g gluten-free flour
35g cocoa powder (make sure it's vegan)
2 tsp baking powder
1 tsp bicarbonate of soda
½ tsp salt
200g unrefined caster sugar
2 tbsp golden syrup
400ml almond milk
60g vegan margarine
1 tsp vanilla extract
100g dark chocolate (make sure it's vegan)

You will also need 12 muffin cases and a muffin baking tin.

Preheat the oven to gas 6/200C/400F

First you need to grind up your chia seeds to make a powder. You can do this in a grinder or blender if you like, but I use a pestle and mortar. Once they are ground mix the seeds and the water together and leave aside until needed.

Sift the flour, cocoa powder, baking powder, bicarb and salt into a large mixing bowl and then add the sugar. Stir these together to make a light brown powder and then make a well in the centre. Next pour the almond milk into the centre and combine using an electric whisk. When you have a smooth batter add the rest of your ingredients, including the chia seed mixture but not the dark chocolate and continue to whisk until the batter is silky smooth.

Chop your dark chocolate into small pieces using a sharp knife and then fold these into the muffin batter. Leave to stand for 10 minutes.

Place your 12 muffin cases into the holes in the muffin tray and then spoon in your batter so that it comes near to the top of the cases. Place in the oven and cook for 25 minutes, or until risen and crisp on top. You can put a cocktail stick into a muffin to check for doneness, but remember that there will be melted chocolate inside so the stick won't always come out clean.

Leave the muffins on a cooling rack and dust with cocoa powder.

WALNUT BRITTLE

Prep time: 5 minutes. Cooking time: 25 minutes. Cooling time: about 90 minutes to completely cool.

Makes 1 tray.

Ingredients:

Vegan margarine for greasing
450g unrefined sugar
175ml cold water
2 tbsp golden syrup
Pinch salt
200g walnut halves

I've always been a big fan of peanut brittle, until I tried walnut brittle. Now I'm a big fan of that. The walnuts add an extra creaminess that peanuts don't have. I have kept the walnuts as halves, rather than chopping them up. This is for aesthetics, but also so that you don't end up with a cloudy toffee when you come to mix in the nuts, which a lot of crumbs would produce.

You are looking to heat the toffee to the 'hard crack' point, which lies somewhere between 146-154°C. This is the point at which the toffee will become hard and brittle when cooled. A sugar thermometer is the best tool for this (I got one on Amazon), or a regular food thermometer will also work fine. If you have neither, it takes about 20 minutes of simmering to get to this point. To test it you can drop a tiny amount into a cup of water. It will immediately harden. Remember to be extra careful when handling hot toffee.

Once the toffee reaches this point and you turn off the heat, it will begin to harden very quickly. For this reason, you want to stir in the nuts with the heat still going and have your lined baking sheet ready to pour the mixture straight into. Trust me, even as you're levelling it out on the sheet it will be hardening and become quite a difficult task. But don't let this put you off as this stuff is amazing.

Also, you'll want to grease both sides of the greaseproof paper with vegan margarine, or you'll have a hell of a job getting the paper off the toffee afterwards.

Method:

Grease a baking sheet with half of the margarine, line the sheet with grease-proof paper and then grease the top of the paper as well with the remaining half.

Put the sugar and water into a saucepan and bring to boiling point. Add the golden syrup and salt and simmer for 20 minutes, or until the toffee reaches the 'hard crack point' of around 150°C.

Mix in the walnuts while the heat is still going (please be careful, this stuff is hot), then pour immediately onto the lined baking sheet. Spread it out using the back of a spoon so that the walnuts are evenly distributed, and the toffee reaches the edges of the tray. Allow to cool completely before touching. Peel the paper off as soon as it is cool and break up to serve.

BLACKBERRY RISOTTO

Cooking time: about 45 minutes

Serves 4.

Ingredients:

1 tbsp coconut oil
250g risotto rice
1 litre oat milk, heated either in a pan or microwave
¼ tsp ground nutmeg
½ tsp ground cinnamon
150g unrefined sugar
200g blackberries, fresh or frozen, plus a few extra to garnish
4 tbsp coconut yoghurt
1 tbsp coconut nectar (maple syrup is also fine)
Drizzle of dairy-free cream to garnish

Risottos don't just have to be savoury, there are plenty that you can make for dessert as well. Blackberries are perfect for a dessert risotto because of their vibrant colour and sweet taste. They are also extremely abundant in the autumn, and if you're the foraging type you can get them for free. This dish is made in exactly the same way as a regular risotto, with the building up of the liquid as the rice cooks, only here we're using oat milk instead of stock. Just like stock, you will want to heat the milk before you start adding it to the rice, otherwise each time you add some the whole dish will cool down. You will also need to stay with the pot as you are cooking, or at least nearby, as the rice absorbs the moisture quickly, so you only have to turn your back for a short time to end up with a dry pan.

Risottos are best served straight away, but if you do want to keep this for later, then I would suggest refrigerating it as soon as possible and adding more milk, or even dairy-free cream, when you are heating it back up. Otherwise it will be too dry.

Method:

Heat the oil in a large pan or wok (wide, shallower pans are better for this than narrow deep ones). Fry the rice for about 3 minutes on a medium heat, stirring often to prevent sticking or burning. Add about 150ml of the milk. It will start to bubble and disappear immediately. Stir it a little and, when the milk has nearly been absorbed, add another 150ml or so. Put in the nutmeg and cinnamon, stir and allow the

241

milk to mostly absorb.

Keep going in this manner: adding a little milk, stirring a bit and letting it absorb. When you are halfway through the milk, add the sugar and stir in. When you have about 200ml of milk left add the blackberries, remembering to leave some back for garnishing. Once all the milk is in and nearly absorbed you can put in the yoghurt and coconut nectar (or syrup, if using). Stir in and taste to see if the rice is cooked. If it needs a little longer you can always add a splash more milk to keep the dish going.

The whole thing will take about 45 minutes in total for the rice to fully cook. Once the rice is cooked, leave to stand for 5 minutes or so before serving, then divide into 4 bowls, drizzle with dairy-free cream and top with some blackberries.

RICE PUDDING

Prep time: 5 minutes.
Cooking time: about 90 minutes.

Serves 4

Ingredients:

50g vegan margarine
200g pudding rice
½ tsp cinnamon
¼ tsp nutmeg
¼ tsp allspice
1.5 litres rice milk
150g unrefined sugar
3 tbsp coconut nectar (golden syrup is also fine)
200ml vegan cream.

If there is a dish filled with nostalgia, then it is rice pudding. A glorious comfort food, a taste steeped in childhood memories and a dessert, thankfully, that is easy to make vegan. If you have a cast iron casserole dish, then you can make this recipe without having to use an extra saucepan as the dish can be put straight onto the stove as well as in the oven. If you don't, then simply make it in a saucepan and transfer it to an oven dish when it is time to put it in the oven. If you can't find coconut nectar, then golden syrup will do just fine.

Method:

Preheat the oven to gas 4/180C/350F.

Melt the butter on the stove, either in a casserole dish or in a saucepan. Add the rice and fry for 4-5 minutes, until fully coated in the oil. Stir in the spices, and then add the rice milk, sugar, coconut nectar and vegan cream. Stir and bring to the boil.

Simmer for 10 minutes, stirring frequently, and then either transfer to an oven dish, or place the casserole dish at the bottom of the oven and cook with the lid off for an hour and a quarter to 90 minutes, until the rice pudding has thickened but has not dried out.

Super Easy Vegan Chocolate Mousse

Prep time: 5-10 minutes.
Chill time: 1-2 hours.

Serves 4 (if you're feeling generous!)

Ingredients:

200g dark chocolate, broken into pieces (leave a little for grating at the end)
1 x 400g block firm tofu, pressed
150ml vegan cream
150g dark brown sugar
1 tbsp cacao powder
2 tsp vanilla extract
150ml almond milk (added 50ml at a time)

Who doesn't love the decadent feel of a spoonful of chocolate mousse on the tongue?

Well, you can have one setting in the fridge a few minutes after you start making it, and that's what we're going to do here. For this recipe you'll need a microwave to melt the chocolate (unless you want to do it the traditional way with a pan of water and a bowl), and a good blender to make sure you get a smooth mixture.

Method:

First put most of your chocolate in a microwavable bowl, saving some for grating later, and heat for 1 ½ to 2 minutes until mostly melted. When there are just a few solid cubes left you can stir it to melt the rest.

Next drain your tofu by wrapping it in a clean tea towel, putting it on a chopping board and putting a heavy pan on top of it. Leave both the chocolate and the tofu for 5 minutes.

Put the tofu, cream, sugar, cacao powder and vanilla extract into the blender and blend until as smooth as you can get it. Pour in your cooled chocolate and blend again. The mixture will thicken up at this point. Now add the almond milk 50ml at a time, blending between each addition, until you come up with a thick but slightly pourable mousse mixture.

Once your mixture is completely smooth, pour or spoon into serving dishes, cover and leave in the fridge for an hour or two to set. When ready to serve, grate some more dark chocolate over the top.

WHOLE WHEAT APPLE CRUMBLE

Prep time: 20-30 minutes.
Cooking time: 35-40 minutes.

Serves 4-6

Ingredients:

For the Apple Base:
1.2 kg apples, peeled, sliced and soaking in cold water
2 tbsp groundnut oil
200g soft brown sugar.

For the Crumble Topping:
250g whole wheat flour
80g rolled oats
150g soft brown sugar
3 tbsp ground flaxseeds
150g vegan margarine, plus extra for greasing.

This is a bit of a cheeky way to get a little more fibre into your diet, and I certainly wouldn't recommend it on a daily basis, but it's a tiny spin on the traditional apple crumble we all grew up with. I've used whole wheat flour, rolled oats and a couple of spoons of ground flaxseeds. This gives a delicious overall nutty flavour to the recipe without actually adding any nuts. The apples are pan-fried first for about 8-10 minutes, which helps to remove any excess moisture from them prior to baking. I add the sugar to the apples while they are still in the pan, caramelising it before putting the apples into the oven dish. Don't be afraid to pile the crumble topping on heavily, so that it more than covers the apples. There's enough flavour here to go around.

Method:

Preheat the oven to gas 6/200C/400F and grease an oven dish with some of the vegan margarine.

Completely drain the apples, getting off as much water as you can. Heat the oil in a large frying pan or wok and sauté the apples for 8-10 minutes. If the apples release a lot of water, then this is the opportunity to drain it off before baking them. Add the sugar to the apples and cook for a minute longer, until the sugar caramelises. Remove from the heat and set aside.

Put all the crumble ingredients into a large mixing bowl, including the margarine, and work through with your fingers until you get a rough breadcrumb texture. Empty the apples into the oven dish and sprinkle the crumble on top, making sure there is about a centimetre or so of crumble over the apples. You might have a little crumble remaining, depending on the size of your dish. Use a dinner fork to create a rough top to the crumble.

Place at the bottom of the oven and bake for 35-40 minutes, until the crumble has browned on top. Remove and let cool for about 15 minutes before serving.

WATERMELON AND COCONUT SORBET

Prep time: 10 minutes.
Cooking time: 5 minutes.
Freezing time: Up to 12 hours.

Makes about 1.2 litres.

Ingredients:

Juice of 1 lemon
200g golden caster sugar
200g creamed coconut, crumbled
Flesh of half a medium watermelon (about 1kg), deseeded and cut into chunks

Originally created as a pallet cleanser between courses, sorbets have become a refreshing dessert all of their own. The process of freezing is made a little easier if you have an ice cream churner, but I made this sorbet without one. All you have to do is whisk it up every hour or two as it is freezing to prevent any large ice crystals from forming. You will also need to bring it out of the freezer a good 15 minutes or so before serving.

Method:

Put the lemon juice and sugar into a saucepan and melt until you have a syrup. Add the coconut and melt over a gentle heat. The sauce will thicken quickly so you need to stir constantly. Once it is melted, turn off the heat and set aside.

Put the watermelon in a blender and add the coconut syrup. Blend until completely smooth, then pour into a container for freezing. While freezing, whisk the sorbet up every hour or two to prevent crystals from forming. It could take up to 12 hours to freeze properly. Thaw for about 15 minutes before serving.

INDEX OF RECIPES

Printed in Great Britain
by Amazon